Best of Barnes
Granddaddyisms, Wit and Wisdom

Highlights from his Daily Courier columns
2013-2020

by Ron Barnes

All proceeds from the sale of this book go to the **Ron and Betsy Youth Scholarship Foundation** *which strives to introduce high school students to the concept of servant leadership, community responsibility and collaborative problem-solving. Youth leaders are recognized annually and awarded scholarships for their continued education.*

.

Credits:
Section illustrations created by Aspen Herzog.
Photos provided by the Barnes family.

ISBN: 9798704991960

FORWARD

Dr. Ron Barnes is one of the first people I met in the mid-'90s when I first started working in Prescott at The Daily Courier newspaper as copy editor. On one of his visits to then-editor Jim Garner back then, Ron had a humble, matter-of-fact, yet powerful presence in the newsroom.

At that point, he had been writing for the Courier for years. He was already a retired educator and businessman who wrote columns for the Courier from January 1989 to January 2004. As I related in my Friday Catchall column on June 7, 2013, Ron had penned two columns a week for 15 years, to which he told me, "My Lord, that's over 1,500 columns!"

That very week in 2013 he came back into the fold, having told me: "I have things I want to write, things I want people to know ... and I will do it for free for you."

I could not say no, not because of the cost but because of his wisdom and clarity. And from June 2013 to October 2020, he added weekly columns for about four years, then shifted to every other week – roughly 300 columns total – following the theme of "The Human Condition."

In all, his columns spanned more than 30 years.

Ron has impacted the Quad Cities community and residents greatly – through many contributions; he worked at Prescott College, retiring in 1985; founded Prescott Area Leadership in 1990, for people who wanted to improve their leadership skills to help shape the future of central Yavapai County; assisted in obtaining funding for Youth Count, to support the young people of the county; and went on to assist in founding a local Boys & Girls Club, MatForce to help reduce substance abuse, as well as founding the Hungry Kids program to provide weekly meals for children in area schools.

His has been a lifelong dedication to youth, leadership and community action.

And he related tidbits, little gems of knowledge, in each of his newspaper columns.

One from November 2014, "Say it today, regret it tomorrow," was true to its headline in which he ended with his personal favorite: "The world will little note nor long remember what we say here, but it can never forget what they did here." We do remember, Mr. Lincoln.

Ron also spoke to us through his writings, as though we were his children, under headlines of "The rise and fall of blatherers," "Not-so-old words," "Thoughts about truth," "Celebrating the moms," and, certainly, is "Granddaddyisms."

i

In one of the latter, he wrote to his first grandson, "You have been given the gift of life, honor it; … the gift of a mind, develop it; … the gift of a body, love it; … the gift of spirit, cherish it; … the gift of a heart, strengthen it; … the gift of a personality, expand it; … the gift of imagination, nurture it; the gift of wonder, cultivate it; … the gift of love, propagate it; … the gift of dreams, pursue it; … (and) the gift of family, treasure it."

For it is within family that we realize and celebrate the essence of our being, he stated.

Yes, with these simple truths, Ron has guided us over the years and I can think of no one better to have written these columns.

He has been like a voice of conscience, and I imagine a little Ron Barnes sitting on my shoulder whispering in my ear, accompanying me, instructing me through my word choices and daily decisions.

We should all have such a shepherd to help us navigate life's challenges.

In his final column he concluded with, "I am a very fortunate and fulfilled man."

Thank you, Ron, and God bless. We are better for your tutelage too.

*- Tim Wiederaenders, senior news editor for **The Daily Courier***

ACKNOWLEDGMENTS

Ron Barnes, the author of this volume, has had many passions in his life. They include becoming a collegiate tennis champion, promoting higher education as both a professor and administrator, facilitating and participating in scholar exchanges during the civil rights movement, and advising corporate leaders on how to realize their full potential. By his side through so many of his adventures has been his greatest love, his wife Betsy, whom he refers to as "my Beloved".

In 1964, Ron chaired the Commission on Higher Education of the Negro for the National Council of Churches. During the summer of 1964, he was a Visiting Professor at Tuskegee Institute in Tuskegee, Alabama.

A long-time resident of Prescott, Arizona, Ron's role in the community has ranged from college administration, sponsor of community tennis tournaments, advocate for treatment of learning disabilities and regular Sunday columnist for The Daily Courier newspaper for over 30 years. He launched the Youth Count organization that brought and coordinated resources for youth development to Yavapai County and started the Community Garden in Prescott and Prescott Valley to help address hunger in the communities. Combining both these concerns, Ron established the Hungry Kids Project devoted to providing weekend take-home meals to children whose school breakfasts and lunches may be their only meals during the week. At time of publication, this program is in its 11th year.

One of the principal underpinnings of Ron's life of action and achievement has been the concept of servant leadership. It is his firm belief that true leadership looks always toward the common good, the empowerment of others to grow into their best selves, and rejects decision-making based primarily on personal gain and aggrandizement.

To promote such enlightened leadership, Ron founded Prescott Area Leadership, a program combining business skills training with in-depth exploration of local communities' institutions, culture and needs. In addition to conducting the year-long educational program, each year PAL honors local community members exemplifying the qualities of servant leadership in a public awards ceremony.

Another natural outgrowth of Ron's interest in youth and leadership was establishment of the Prescott Area Youth Leadership Academy which strives to introduce high schoolers to the concepts of servant leadership, community responsibility and collaborative problem-solving. Youth leaders are also recognized annually and awarded scholarships for their continued education. All proceeds from the sale of this book go to the Ron and Betsy Barnes Youth Scholarship Foundation established for this purpose.

It comes as no surprise to those who know him that Ron's legacy includes this book in which he's compiled a selection of his columns encouraging those in later life to continue growing into their best selves. Proving that servant leadership has no age limits, Ron gently, sometimes humorously, and always insightfully inspires his readers to blossom as grandparents, community members and human beings.

- Alex Piacenza, Daily Courier columnist and PAL graduate

CONTENTS

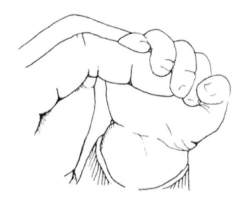

GRANDDADDYISMS

Dylan and his Granddaddy Ron

"Granddaddyisms" pass along wisdom

Beginning in June 2008, I began writing granddaddyisms for our grandson, Dylan. The purpose was to help him understand himself and the life he was living as a teenager. He was 16 when I began these communications and 18 when I penned the final one. I told him to respond if he had questions or comments he wanted to share, but not because he thought I expected him to. Sometimes he called or wrote, sometimes not.

Perhaps some of you who have teenagers of your own or grandsons or granddaughters coping with turbulent adolescent challenges might find some of what I wrote to Dylan of interest. Anyhow, from time to time, I'll share with you a few granddaddyisms. I hope you enjoy them.

Try to never lose your sense of wonder, Dylan. It's the only thing that will continue to dazzle you, no matter your age. It's imbedded in what you see, hear, smell, touch and taste. As you grow older, some of life becomes old-hat. Sort of a 'been there, done that' syndrome. The antidote to that kind of boredom or malaise is to activate that childlike wonder. But it's tough to do if you haven't kept yours alive and fresh. So always nurture the child in you. Each year you age, that nurturance becomes more important.

Attitude may not be the most important element in your development, but it's close. You view the world not as it is, but as you are. Your attitude toward reality determines your perspective on life. Your attitude is the root of your perceptions and perspectives. The more positive you are about your life, the more positive your life will become. Live in a way that gives you joy and a sense of peace - a way that makes sense to you and those who love you. But if you live as if the world is watching you, you may discover that you are the unhappiest person on the funny farm.

Intelligence is no guarantee of wisdom, just as sensitivity is no guarantee of compassion. Purpose, intent and commitment come into the equation big-time. I believe compassion is more critical to your development than intelligence.

If you want to become acquainted with a person, listen to what he or she says. If you want to know a person, pay attention to what he or she does. Too many people say one thing and do another. It's an individual's behavior that best identifies who they are, not their words.

If you get annoyed easily, you either need an attitude adjustment or a good night's sleep.

Friendship begins to become a trusting relationship when you share feelings. Until you are able to share joy and sorrow, elation and pain, hope and despair, your real self remains hidden. You have to be able to risk true openness.

To make friends, learn to ask questions. No matter our age, we respond favorably to people who ask us what we think about this issue or that, how we feel about things. But be sure you are sincere. You must want to hear their opinion or get their reaction to your question. Most everyone can spot phonies.

To live a rich life, Dylan, communication must transcend 'you and me.' The focus must be 'us.' Simply listening to what one says while thinking of a response isn't good enough. Until you look inside yourself and reply with whatever feelings are swirling around in there, the communication remains outside the boundaries of self. It's just words.

Emulate, don't imitate. Pay attention to people you like and admire, then learn from their strengths and best qualities. But don't try to become them. You can't. And if you try, you'll risk losing the special and unique qualities that make you who you are. Emulation enables you to retain those qualities and characteristics.

Some reflections for my grandson

When our first grandson was born some 27 years ago, I sent him this page of reflections. Of course I didn't expect he would be able to read this until he was two, maybe three!

You have been given the gift of life.
Honor it. Respect all other inhabitants, people, animals, plants. You have a legacy and responsibility to all future children to leave this planet better than you found it. Do for them what you wish others had done for you.

You have been given the gift of a mind.
Develop it. It will become what you want it to be. Use it well and often, and never permit others to gain control of it, but be aware that many will try. Learn as much as you can about the world and yourself and you will be prepared for the inevitable difficult challenges in the years ahead.

You have been given the gift of a body.
Love it. You will have it for life so take care of it. Feed it nourishing meals, exercise it, make judicious guardianship a priority, but avoid becoming a health zealot. Your body will serve you well if you respect its basic requirements.

You have been given the gift of spirit.
Cherish it. Try to retain the blissful, free fervor and energy you possess as a child. Never lose your passion for the moment or your zeal to live fully in every encounter. Retain your child-like enthusiasm and your world will be forever rich.

You have been given the gift of a heart.
Strengthen it. Encourage it to reach out to others, put it in the middle of all interactions, and let its influence be guided by your instincts. Understand that it will be wounded at times, is susceptible to suffering and pain, but to live without its fullness or restrict its outreach is no life at all.

You have been given the gift of a personality.
Expand it. No other in the world will be like it. So develop its uniqueness, treat it as a flower that needs daily attention if it is to reach its full beauty, and let it shine brightest in the company of others.

You have been given the gift of imagination.
Nurture it. As a child it will enable you to visit enchanted lands, climb great mountains and invent magic fantasies. As an adult, it will encourage you to go beyond the narrow, restrictive images of the present to create pictures of a better, more humane world in which, hopefully, your children

will live.

You have been given the gift of wonder.

Cultivate it. You live in a world with wondrous beauty, incredible resources and awe-inspiring miracles. Use your innate curiosity in ways that will permit it to grow so that in your twilight years you can still be surprised, astounded and delighted.

You have been given the gift of love.

Propagate it. Encourage and strengthen it so that you can become a selfless advocate of its power. Let no one take it from you, nor permit others to weaken your commitment to share it as widely as your concern for humanity dictates.

You have been given the gift of dreams.

Pursue it. Dreams give meaning, flavor and substance to your life. Without dreams, life is drab, uninspired and spiritless. Significant accomplishments are preceded by momentous dreams. So dream great things, my grandson, and then strive to make them real.

You have been given the gift of family.

Treasure it. Glory in its unequivocal, inextinguishable love. Seek comfort within it as needed, contribute to it your talents and skills, share within it your concerns and questions, and in your maturity, pass along your pledge to sustain and glorify its sanctity. For it is within family that we realize and celebrate the essence of our being.

Sharing wisdom with the next generation

Always remember, Dylan, that kindness, tenderness and love have a great healing power. Share these feelings with others whenever you can and your life will be more beautiful. And it's likely you will receive a return on your investment.

Dylan, try not to give away your control. Example: "You make me angry!" That's baloney. A more honest statement is, "I have permitted you to make me angry." No one can take control over you without your permission. No one can make you angry unless you permit them to do so. Hold on to your control. Don't give it away to others. And don't blame someone for something you are doing to yourself.

Okay, listen up, Dylan. This is about you and what you are experiencing. It's about the small war of independence all teenagers fight during their teenage years. Adolescence is essentially a period when youngsters your age struggle to become more independent as a person and less dependent on parents. Since this is all new to you, you're not very well prepared to handle it. No teenager is. So maybe this short exegesis will help:

Becoming more independent is a necessary step to adulthood. Adolescence is a time when your identification with parents diminishes and when the opinions and behavior of peers elevate in importance. It's a time when youngsters yearn for freedom and want to be regarded as young adults. "You're treating me like a child" is a familiar response to parental authority.

For teenagers freedom takes many forms. For you, it's a car, so you can have the freedom of driving to your destination instead of depending on others to chauffeur you; it's money that you earn so you can spend it or save it as you wish; it's jobs that show you and others that you are mature and responsible and can function as a young adult. To put it plainly, Dylan, you are handling your adolescence in a pretty mature way. I am proud of you.

Look around and you'll see young people who aren't making this transition very well. Some test their limits and rebel against adult authority by turning to drugs, alcohol, tobacco, tattoos, piercing, etc. They are engaging in behavior that thumbs their noses at parents and the adult world while attempting to appear adult-like, not realizing they are hurting themselves in the process. Their behavioral choices often have unfortunate consequences they will have to live with for the rest of their lives.

You see, Dylan, there is a psychological issue that characterizes adolescent behavior. It's this: At the root of dependency is anger. A baby is totally dependent on parents for survival. Young children are also dependent. But it's in the teen years that adolescents begin to feel, and want to be, less dependent and more independent. When parents say things that cause them to feel dependent, they tend to become angry. The fact is there is nothing wrong with anger; it's how one handles anger that can cause problems. Road rage is a dangerous way to handle anger. So is hitting someone or taking drugs or throwing a rock through a window. Yelling at a parent or a sibling isn't all that positive a response either, and it has the unfortunate result of hurting them. What you need to do is find acceptable, positive ways of discharging your anger - ways that don't hurt those you love who love you. For me, it was primarily hitting a ball on a tennis court. For you it may be running or driving your tractor or even a hard game of ping-pong.

The challenge for parents is to gradually assist their youngster to become less dependent and more independent. It's not easy - for any parent - just as it isn't easy for teenagers like you to ease into independence. Be patient, be understanding, be loving, and learn how to control and express your anger in positive, healthy ways. I think you'll be happier if you do.

Life lessons we all can learn from

Dylan, learn the meaning of serendipity, then be open to it - for the rest of your life. If you do this, your life will be richer and you will more likely experience personal fulfillment and happiness. I guarantee it.

The richer your imagination, the richer your world.

If you wish to earn the respect and admiration of seniors, refrain from addressing them as "guys" and respond to them with "yes" rather than "yeah." In the South, you will frequently hear them addressed as "Sir" and "Ma'am." These are also terms of respect in the rest of the U.S., if not most of the world. Avoid saying "Me and Austin are going..." Stick with "Austin and I." The other person gets priority over you. Use these words when communicating with folks and people's admiration of you will increase immeasurably. You are getting to an age where you will need the respect of your elders.

One of the marks of maturity is how you handle things you don't want to do. You are going to learn that there are a lot of competent people in the world. These are folks who know how to do things and do them well. They do quality work and care about what they do. We benefit from their efforts. I want you to be competent in whatever you do. But while the world functions better when competence is present, there is a higher level I hope you will seek. I want you to be not only competent, but to be significant as well.

To live a significant life, you must want and try to make a positive difference in the lives of others. It is significant people who make our lives - and the world - better, not by what they do (competence), but by who they are.

They are the people we respect and admire and try to emulate.

Be an optimistic person, Dylan. But do become aware that you can't leap a canyon in two jumps.

Want to be successful in your life and work? Then never underestimate the value of perseverance.

If you value friends and your reputation, keep your word. Do what you say you will do and trust will follow.

Increasingly you'll discover that what you know you owe to the questions you ask. Continue to be curious, Dylan. It's one of your best traits.

Be aware that alibis are self-enhancing rationalizations connected to a self-serving imagination.

You don't know this yet, Dylan, and are unlikely to appreciate it now, but one of the best gifts your parents have given you is a map. It's not like the maps you are familiar with. In this map, you decide the destination. What your folks have done is to provide you ways to reach that destination safely and establish directions that will enrich your journey. They have given you interesting things to look for and pointed out possible challenges you may encounter along the way. They have taught you how to appreciate the countryside you are passing through and suggested ways to learn from those you meet. They have assisted you to understand the environmental changes you will likely experience - and so much more. In other words, they have done a fine job of preparing you for your life's journey. In time, you will want to thank them. For now, you might consider just telling them you appreciate the map. They won't have a clue what you're talking about, so just smile and look goofy. You do both of these things so well.

Humor, perspective go a long way in life

If there is one thing you'll need in life to maintain a balance and a perspective that will enable you to cope with difficult times and loss and tough challenges, it's a sense of humor. Nurture yours, Dylan. Look for the funny, listen to what makes people laugh, pay attention to comedians, read humorous articles and books. Without a sense of humor, life can be a downer and days can be long and tedious and unnecessarily gray. Learn to approach life with a smile, with an expectation that there is a hidden, comedic event or happening around the next corner. Look for humor and it's likely to emerge.

Almost as important as developing and maintaining a rich sense of humor is the need to nurture a sense of moral outrage. There is so much injustice and evil and suffering in the world that needs attention. Keep a fire in your belly; never become a dispassionate observer; never anesthetize yourself or become a cynic. Care, Dylan, care. Then try to do whatever you can to bring forth justice and fight evil and alleviate suffering. And keep in mind the words of St. Augustine: "Hope has two beautiful daughters; their names are Anger and Courage - anger at the way things are, and courage to see that they do not remain the way they are."

You've no doubt heard that old saw practice makes perfect, right? Well, it's an okay message, but it's also fiddle-faddle. Some people will tell you that only perfect practice makes perfect. That's a little better, but not much. The reality is, we are flawed individuals, and 'perfect' simply isn't in the cards. None of us is perfect, nor are we going to be. So just try to do your best. Concentrate on what you are doing, give it your best shot and move on. People who think they can be perfect in whatever are in for a whole heap of frustration and disappointment.

Be very slow to accept the cliché "Everything happens for the best." Or this one, "Everything happens for a reason." I've never been able to explain these careless conclusions to people who are homeless or to kids who wake up each morning wondering whether they will have any food to eat that day or to parents whose children have been murdered by people with guns, or... well, you get the point. There are way too many unexamined bromides floating around out there.

Understand, Dylan, that everyone is ignorant, just in different ways. There is so much to learn in so many subjects and so much knowledge accumulated in the world that it's understandable we are ignorant. Most of us know a little bit about a little bit. While we should acknowledge our ignorance, we don't have to be stupid, which means pretending we know more than we do, or not being interested in learning or improving ourselves, or being self-satisfied, or lacking curiosity about the world we live in, or believing our education ends when we leave school. Smart folks know there is always much more to learn so they are dedicated to being lifelong learners. They know they rarely have clear answers to the important questions. They are slow to make up their minds about tough, complex issues.

Be wary of those folks who try to tell you what is right. Be slow to embrace cocksure individuals. There are too many people who live by the motto, 'My mind is made up; don't bother me with the facts.' Of course, they have a right to their beliefs and the right to live in their encapsulated world. But, too frequently, they feel compelled to try to persuade the rest of us that their truths are what we should accept. These people are usually strangers to critical thinking and to a liberating education which puts emphasis on questions, doubt and curiosity.

The more complex the world becomes, the more people want simplistic answers. They will also prefer a sheltered existence where they don't have to think about tough questions and difficult matters. These folks often become suckers for hucksters who are happy to do their thinking for them while providing them with simple, rigid instructions on what to think and believe. Be joyful, Dylan, that your life journey has, so far, been lit by the lights of learning, not by the darkness of dogma. You are a lucky young man. I hope you realize that.

Coolness, 'lex talionis' are social traps

Let me say a few words about being 'cool'. What's cool to teenagers may not be cool in the long run. Too many adolescents live exclusively in the present without realizing there may be significant consequences for their daily actions and behavior. Some mistakes are erased by time, but some aren't. Be cool, extract fun from the moment, but be smart enough to realize that choices made today may have huge consequences tomorrow. Oh, and two questions for you to ponder: Does cool mean there is no warmth and passion inside? Can cool lead to being frigid?

Dylan responded to this in a positive, insightful way. Here was my response to him: Great insight on 'cool,' Dylan. You're right. It changes among the young, especially with each group. What's cool for some isn't for others. And yes, it's hard sometimes not to be cool depending on how others define the term. Stand on your values, do what you believe is right, and you'll be fine. Traveling with people who share your values is a good way to go. And you have apparently found those kinds of friends. I'm proud of you.

You are going through a period in your life when peers assume more importance in your life than parents. You want their approval more than you do the approval of parents, which you already have. This is a normal process of becoming independent of parents and less dependent on them. It's what teenagers go through. It's called 'growing up.' One of the ways you will know that adolescence is coming to an end is when what peers think of you no longer matters so much. It's when you become the primary playwright of your life script. It's when you begin acknowledging 'I am what I am' (Popeye) and no longer feel it is necessary to be who others say you are.

Here is a major principle of human behavior that you can take to the bank. It's called lex talionis, which is a biblical reference meaning "an eye for an eye and a tooth for a tooth." Let me give you a humorous and real example.

When we were living in Ames (1961-1966), we saw a fascinating article in the newspaper. It indicated that the Iowa legislature passed a piece of legislation declaring the sunflower, the state flower of Kansas, a noxious weed. Several weeks later, the Kansas legislature passed legislation declaring the eastern goldfinch, the state bird of Iowa, a public nuisance.

This is a wonderful illustration of lex talionis and juvenile behavior. But it has a serious side. It explains why nations go to war and why people get into fights. It's why people go to court. 'You did it to me, I'll do it to you.' It's the Law of Retaliation. And it happens all the time. In families, in governments, between kids in schoolyards - wherever people come together.

The behavior begins with small babies. Take a bottle away from a baby before he or she is ready and you will likely hear a loud, lusty cry of protest. The next time you approach the baby with a bottle, she will likely slap it away and put on her ugly face. She is saying, "You hurt me, I'll hurt you." Why, I've even seen 16 year-olds retaliate against their parents when they are punished for screwing up. Perhaps you can think of several incidents? Lex talionis - pay attention to it, Dylan. You are going to see examples of it for the rest of your life. In fact during the next two years of high school, you'll probably receive a graduate degree in the subject.

Well, Dylan, as you have discovered there are a great many organizations in society that are high on indoctrination and low on freedom. There are also the reverse. If this issue is important to you, then you will want to learn to ask pertinent questions before committing yourself to membership.

Most of the difficult decisions you will make in your life will require using both your mind and your heart. Your best judgments will involve listening to both.

I may not be able to tell you how to be successful, but I'm pretty sure I know how you can become a failure: Try to please everyone.

Words of wisdom smooth life's roads.

Has anyone ever said to you 'Don't take it to heart?' What they likely mean is that you need not take what they say seriously. But I want to give this admonition another spin. I believe there are a great many things that you will want to take to heart because those thoughts, emotions, passions and feelings that you permit to enter your heart will always be there for you. Whatever trials, misfortunes and adversity you encounter in life can be counterbalanced by the forces of goodness, wholesomeness, integrity, and virtue that has been collected by you and stored in your heart. I want your heart to be full of love, empathy, and compassion. I want it to connect with the hearts of others so that you can feel what they do, and they can experience an attachment that binds them to you. The greatest bond you will experience is when your heart and the heart of another person come together and, in a very real sense, become one. Prepare your heart for this union, Dylan, and your life will be immeasurably blessed.

Dylan, much of your life will involve problem-solving. So I have a suggestion: Try to reduce the problem to the core. Don't enlarge it.

There may not be a more important skill than that of choosing well. The quality of your life will largely hinge on your ability to make good and wise choices.

Here's another lesson that I feel is important for young people your age to understand. Don't compare yourself with others. The 'others' are always going to change. You have some good friends now, but in several years most of them will no longer be your close friends. They will move away or go to college somewhere or get jobs, or you will move away and it's unlikely you will maintain contact with them. I keep in touch with only one of my high school friends and the only thing we share is a few sentences through Christmas cards. My point is that you have to be yourself. It's fine to learn from others; just don't try to be them. Do the best you can do, pursue your goals, live by your values, develop your beliefs, live your life. We are all different. Celebrate your individuality.

One of the important lessons in life is to learn to distinguish between worries and concerns. The former are distressful, the latter have the potential of causing distress. The trick is to not permit concerns to become worries. Try not to enlarge or exaggerate concerns.

Dylan, your life is going to become busier and increasingly complex. College, for instance, is going to mean you will be faced with setting daily priorities and making quick, important decisions. I suggest you become more selective in making choices that move you to action. Try not to let issues beyond your control dominate your day. There will be enough challenges that require your time and attention without you undertaking unnecessary ones.

Lose your capacity to play and your world will lose color. Repress your humor and your emotions will likely wither. Stifle your particular brand of creative play and your perspective will become warped. Ignore the foolishness that surrounds you and your ability to laugh will become impaired. In other words, never let play, a playful attitude, and a playful approach to life become less than a priority.

If you care about a relationship with someone, treat them with honor. To me that means respect and compassion. It means you honor that person's opinions and beliefs. You care about them despite their flaws and imperfections. What they say or do may provoke anger in you, but this is your problem, not theirs. You must learn to handle your anger in a way that does not reflect negatively upon you. If you permit your anger to explode upon them, you have managed your anger poorly. And you have not handled yourself or the other person honorably.

Make each day count, Dylan. That beats the heck out of counting days.

Nurture 'uncommon sense' to succeed

Dylan, here is an important lesson about yourself and other people. Being human, we see what we want to see, hear what we want to hear, and believe what we want to believe. The cliché 'Don't bother me with the facts, my mind is made up' has a lot of truth in it. To carry this a little further, we see things not as they are, but as we are. We process information through our own unique individual filter. Our perceptions of the world are determined by who we are and what we choose to believe, see and hear. Never underestimate this reality.

Nothing of real consequence can be accomplished without passion. Always nurture yours.

I suspect you are probably too old for a short discourse on the birds and bees, so I will move forward and share with you a few thoughts about an important related matter. When two individuals are attracted to one another, a major issue they must deal with is their hormones and the corollary feelings of lust. Here is the catch. Too many young people mistake lust for love. In marriages, over time, the feelings of lust become less intense. If the spouses have equated lust with love, this may cause the individuals to believe that their love is diminishing because their physical responses to one another are less intense. One consequence for many couples is to end their marriages because their love life isn't what it used to be. The fact is, sustaining an intense sexual relationship is challenging as the years accumulate. Here is my point: In a mature relationship a couple gradually realizes that companionship is really the essence of their lives together and this understanding becomes the center and focus of a couple's later years. So, when entering into relationships, look for a person you enjoy being with and who has the character and qualities that go far beyond immediate sensual impressions. In the long run, the determinant of a happy union is this: Will this individual make a good companion for the rest of your days on this planet? You may not feel a certainty, but you can feel a strong probability. And, of course, if I'm still hanging around then, give me a call. I've spent decades with the best companion imaginable. I'll probably have an opinion or two.

As you add years to your age, the people you are likely to respect the most are those who put the common good before their self-interest.

Be aware that common sense is worth possessing, but it IS common. Everyone has a bit of it; some people have more than others. What you should strive to develop is uncommon sense, which is the ability to see what others don't. You should learn to look beyond the surface of the matter, to look for what's different about a situation, to examine the consequences, explore different dimensions, seek out alternative options. Uncommon sense sets a person apart from others. Be uncommon, Dylan.

If you choose your words carefully when presenting an argument, you will never need to shout.

Only fools are self-satisfied. A wise person is never satisfied with himself, his accomplishments or the quality of his life. An individual, man or woman, can always do better.

I believe that wishful thinking is a belief in magic. Too many people sit around waiting for some sort of inspiration that will enable them to accomplish an assignment or suddenly become creative. They prefer to wait for a magical moment rather than commit themselves to the rigorous demand of disciplining their minds, or pursuing the boring requirements of detailed follow-through. During the 15 years that I wrote newspaper columns, I thought about putting this subtitle under my heading of "The Human Condition: The Muse Never Showed Up, So I Had To Write This Stuff Myself."

When you make the right call, you win

During one of our conversations, Dylan asked me what lessons I had learned from my years of playing tournament tennis.

Well, Dylan, I learned a great many lessons when I played the summer tennis circuit back in the late 40s and early 50s, and here is a significant one. My opponent and I were nearing the end of the deciding set when he hit a ball that was very close to the back line. Since we played without linesmen for this match, the umpire couldn't make the call so he asked me if it was good. I replied immediately that it was out. A few moments later, I realized I reacted too quickly. It might have touched the outer part of the line. I was in a serious quandary. I should have replied that I was unsure whether it was in or out and then the umpire would have asked us to replay the point. My call gave me match point. I toweled off to give me a few extra moments to decide what to do. I made the decision to dump his serve into the net, which I did. I felt it was the right thing to do. My opponent raised his racket in a sort of salute which confirmed for me that I had made the right decision. He obviously thought his shot caught the line.

So, Dylan, what was the lesson? It's a big one, and it took me a number of years after this match to draw a larger meaning from this incident. Tennis is about what you do between the lines. But it's not just about the quality of your shots. It's also about character. And here's the major lesson: IN LIFE, THERE WILL ALWAYS BE LINES. And there will always be tough calls to make. I made a bad one and was fortunate that I had an immediate opportunity to correct it. Had I won the match on the next point I would have regretted that victory for the rest of my life. It was a matter of personal integrity. We don't always get that second chance. I think if you are to have a successful, gratifying, personally fulfilling future, you need to play between the lines. Sometimes you will determine those lines but often they will be drawn for you by other people or governments or society. But be assured, the lines exist. You need to figure out where they are and live your life inside of them. That is where the game of life needs to be played. Those individuals who play outside the lines will likely experience difficulty and will often find themselves in trouble.

Being criticized is sometimes very difficult to accept, especially when you believe you did the right thing. The only way I know to avoid criticism is to do nothing. For people like you and me, this is a totally unacceptable alternative.

I'm proud of you for going to your friend's commencement. I'm sure he appreciated you making the effort to attend. Yes, I have delivered a few commencement addresses in my lifetime. Each one quite forgettable, I'm afraid. In researching commencement addresses I discovered that the shortest one ever delivered was by the French philosopher, Andre Gide. His entire speech was this line: "Everything that needs to be said has already been said, but since no one was listening, everything must be said again." For one delirious moment I contemplated repeating this gem, but quickly decided I would receive no fee if I did. Gide, with his reputation, could get away with it, but I had NO reputation so I wisely chickened out.

In studying old commencement addresses I ran across this extraordinary one by Goethe, the great German poet and philosopher. Here it is, in its entirety: 'There are nine requisites for contented living: health enough to make work a pleasure; wealth enough to support your needs; strength enough to battle with difficulties and overcome them; grace enough to confess your sins and forsake them; patience enough to toil until some good is accomplished; charity enough to see some good in your neighbor; love enough to move you to be useful and helpful to others; faith enough to make real the things of God; hope enough to remove all anxious fears concerning the future.' I believe this speech is a keeper!

I want you to think about a statement made by Pope Pius VI. He said "If you want peace, work for justice." It seems to me that this world you and I live in is more concerned with order than with justice. And if I read history correctly, a concern for disorder over injustice seems to produce more of both.

Kind words improve life for everyone

Dylan, here is a goal you may wish to develop. During your lifetime, consider devoting more of your energy and time praising people than finding fault with them. Blaming others or putting them down for their shortcomings or perceived limitations and flaws is a monumental waste of time. Besides, the effort will only add misery to your life. And it certainly won't gain you friends or persuade them to feel positively about you.

Be aware that most people are quick to find fault and slow to commend. Think about yourself. Is it easier for you to criticize or commend? How often do you think about the things your mother, dad, brother or friends do that annoy you or cause you to become angry or provoke you to deliver an unkind reaction or unkind words? Then think about how often you say something positive or loving about them or to them.

When is the last time you told someone you like them or love them or that they mean a lot to you or that they just said or did something that you want to thank them for? Think how you feel when someone says something nice about you. Well, Dylan, people like it when you say positive things about them. And they will like you better when you do. You win friends and the respect of others when you are kind and thoughtful; you lose friends and respect - and sometimes love - when you are unkind and thoughtless.

Be kind and thoughtful and positive, Dylan. Learn to express those feelings to others. Their responses will fill your life with kindness and love and respect. And you will become a happier person. I guarantee it!

• People who consider themselves unlucky are usually victims of their own poor decisions. So they try to rationalize those decisions by calling themselves unlucky. They aren't honest enough to acknowledge that they have screwed up.

• Dylan, never turn your mind or heart or soul over to someone else. They will likely rob you.

• I hope you are still enjoying your music and finding time to play your guitar. Good music - the kind that enriches your senses and brings joy to your soul - has no meanness, sarcasm, hatred, anger or prejudice. It speaks to the best that is in you. It raises your spirit, penetrates your heart with love, and brings joy to your life. Learn to appreciate symphonies by Beethoven, Mozart and Bach. And someday I hope you will listen to my favorite composer and my all-time favorite composition, "Rhapsody in Blue." And if you like that, listen to "An American in Paris," and

Gershwin's folk opera "Porgy and Bess."

• I believe one of life's most important lessons is to understand that all of us are flawed human beings. We are imperfect individuals. What we should attempt to do, of course, is work at identifying and correcting those flaws as opposed to trying to hide them and pretending they don't exist or that no one pays attention to them. As we do this, we should also work at developing our strengths. You, Dylan, have particular gifts (abilities, talents and skills) that contribute to you becoming a good, strong individual. A good life is earned by the person who minimizes flaws (limitations) and maximizes strengths. You might consider making two columns on a page and listing them.

• I think it's likely, Dylan, that you are going to do some really dumb things in your life. Everyone does. Learn from your mistakes and try not to repeat them. Then move on. It's only the future you can do anything about. The past is history.

• You will learn - if you haven't already - that those individuals who are dedicated to furthering their self-interests are often blind to the needs of others.

• Dylan, you are a plural noun. You are you, of course, but you are also the product of your parents, your brother, your grandparents and friends. In other words, others have shaped your identity and will continue to do so. We will always be a part of you. You are never really alone.

A few examples of 'living the Good Life'

"What do you write about, Granddaddy?"

"Well, I like to think that I write mostly about things that matter."

That snippet of a conversation with a granddaughter occurred years ago, but only recently was recovered by me in a memory flash.

But my granddaughter's question is still relevant. And so I will try to respond because in a sense what really matters are those conversations each of us has with ourselves and with others about issues and questions that attempt to explain what is important in our lives.

And while there are many different themes to examine, I believe one of the most critical falls under the heading of "The Good Life." What are the significant components that make up "The Good Life" that most of us would like to live?

Well, of course, there are the critical personal issues like good health, the love of a mate, the respect of friends, a job one enjoys and a satisfactory income along with basic essentials like clean water, nutritious food, adequate shelter, etc. But I'm more focused on those qualities or characteristics that define who we are and what we do with our lives.

So, what is a "Good Life?"

Here are some of my thoughts; by no means a complete list. I hope you will provide some of your own.

• It's living a life that enables you to achieve the priorities you have set for yourself.

• It's living in a wholesome environment in which your children can be raised.

• It's living in a community in which you can feel safe.

• It's having a caring and nurturing relationship with nature.

• It's a life that involves intimate and positive relationships within a loving family and within a supportive community.

• It's becoming active within the community to create a more caring and just society.

• It's being able to define for yourself the nature of your success, the meaning of freedom and the requirements of equal justice for all citizens.

• It's living in a society that lives up to a commitment to social equality.

• It's the freedom to express yourself against all constraints and conventions.

• It's being able to define who you are and become who you wish to be.

• It's being aware that self-examination is the key to insight which is the road to wisdom.

• It's living a lifestyle that is intentional and reflects values consistent with your ideals.

• It's exploring your life story and discovering it is making sense.

• It means becoming your own person without denying the important role parents have played in the development of your life.

• It's understanding that self-discovery is never accomplished alone, but only through interacting in relationships, groups, associations and communities.

• It's understanding that your connectedness to others is essential to your happiness, self-esteem and moral worth.

• It's acknowledging your interdependency.

• It's developing an attitude and approach to the world that is liberating because it gets you in touch with your own wants and interests, freed from the artificial constraints of social roles and the guilt-inducing demands of parents and other authorities.

• It's understanding the moral component of friends who help you become a better person and who will forgive your failings but not excuse them.

• A good life is primarily influenced by the success you have in your life's work, the service you render to your community, and for many, strong spiritual convictions.

• It's becoming aware that the goodness of society depends upon the goodness of individuals.

Play up strengths, forget fears

Dylan, many adults have a need to ask young people what they want to be when they grow up. This well-meaning question really seeks to find out what occupation you plan to pursue. Please know that your granddaddy is more interested in the question, "Who do you want to become as a person?" The quality of your life and character takes a higher priority than the work-life you select. Your choice of an occupation is important, but it shouldn't be an end in itself. It is the road you travel that enables you to earn a living. But the quality of your life is also predicated on the contribution you make in serving others and making the world a better place. This can be accomplished, of course, through your occupation. But a good life is also the result of who you are and what you do with all your gifts, abilities and skills. Fortunate is the individual whose work enables him or her to contribute to the welfare of society and whose non-work life is also devoted to making a positive difference in the life of others.

* Be wary of cocksure people; they tend to possess petrified beliefs and opinions.

* The longer I live, the clearer it is to me that one of the most important roots of love is forgiveness. And perhaps the most important lesson about forgiveness is that the opportunity to forgive is always before you. Not a bad lesson for someone your age either, Dylan.

* As you age, you're going to remember these years when you were living at home as a teenager. What kind of memories will you have? Pleasant ones? Unpleasant ones? Will they be memories that provoke you to wish you had done things differently? For instance, Austin is going to be your younger brother for as long as you live. Are you now building the kind of caring relationship that will make him want to be close and supportive of you when you are both adults? What about your relationship with your mother? Are you the kind of loving, caring son that will make you proud of yourself when you remember these years when you are 30, 40, 50 and 60? You don't get a second chance to make up for what you do or don't do during these years, Dylan. So try to get it right. Now.

* Try to understand that a little lie or a little cheating is like a little bit of pregnancy; it's there and likely to get bigger.

* The road to mental health is paved, in part, with coping skills and resilience, not with senseless worries. I recall, Dylan, when I was you age I worried needlessly about my physical appearance. Little flaws were exaggerated and gained an inordinate amount of my attention. How utterly useless and unnecessary were my concerns. Everyone else my age paid

little or no attention to my perceived flaws because they were so focused on their own. So, learn this significant lesson: You are not the focus of their lives. Center on your strengths, try to minimize your limitations, but don't permit yourself to get worked up about them.

* Who you are is far more important to your friends than how you look. Your demeanor - smiles, interest in their lives, sincerity in communications, and self-confidence - will make you an admired friend and companion. Caring about people, along with not taking yourself too seriously, is the real basis for friendship. Try to become less self-centered, a tough challenge for someone your age, but worth the effort.

* Perhaps the best measure of a life is not what you have done for others, but what others have done because of you. Infusing a spark or your spirit or an idea into another person insures your immortality. Something of you lives on in others.

Child-like joy is key to happiness

• Your life is filled with rich experiences. Each day you have them, each class is an experience, each assignment, each contact with your friends. Your mission trip last year was a rich experience. Your upcoming trip to Uganda will be a major experience. In other words, your entire life will be one experience after another. But what is important for you to understand is that it's your response to each experience that really matters. It's what you learn that will determine what kind of life you have. The quality of your life will be enriched by what you do, but only if you actively seek to make them rich experiences.

The fateful fact is, most people do not take advantage of their life experiences. They have them, just as you do, but they fail to take the time, or make the effort, to examine the consequences of what they have done, or consider the applications the experiences have for their life. And they fail to apply what they have learned. They simply go from one experience to the next without pausing to reflect on what they have learned. You must ask yourself what meaning, if any, each experience has for me, Dylan Clark. Some experiences may not teach you squat; they are just simple experiences. So don't expect great insights or a significant lesson. Pick your spots. But do take a little time to reflect what - if anything - you have learned. Education isn't confined to schools. Your education on this planet is finished when you take your final breath. Learning is how you achieve your education. You will learn from your experiences if you choose to do so.

• Many profound thoughts and truths are wrapped in humor. Here is a favorite of mine, courtesy of Woody Allen: "More than any time in history mankind faces a crossroads. One path leads to despair and utter hopelessness, the other to extinction. Let us pray we have the wisdom to choose correctly."

• Perhaps one of the most important questions a person your age can ask himself (or herself) is this one: "Are you becoming the type of individual you will be happy living with for the rest of your life?"

• Let me suggest a perspective for you to consider. You're young, you're discovering, you're learning what works for you, what doesn't, what you can do and can't do. But what is really important is to understand that STAYING YOUNG is an inside job all the way - from the beginning to the end. I am a mature man, yet I still have within me a young boy's heart. When you are my age, I hope you will have one as well. That results from developing an attitude and a choice of a lifestyle that only you can make.

Your body will inevitably age, but your approach to life doesn't need to. Some people get old before their time. Their mental and emotional processes age, they become overly cautious in their choices, too serious about their lives, they stop having fun, stop taking risks, they atrophy intellectually and emotionally, and become the type of person who is no fun to be around. Their lives lack excitement. Your choice, Dylan, is whether to stay alive and actively pursue life with enthusiasm and excitement or take life as it comes and let it control you. It's the difference between being proactive or reactive. Be proactive, Dylan. It's a lot more fun.

• I believe it is difficult to stay mentally and emotionally healthy if you don't cultivate and possess a sense of play. Try to retain a child-like joy and never lose the ability to have fun playing games.

Uncommon sense can change world

• Dylan, to a significant degree, we are what we appreciate. For instance, some people love ornamentation. They like to wear baubles that, in their opinion, make them attractive. Some prefer tattoos, another external statement of who they think they are. (Of course, as the "tattooists" mature, many of them regret their youthful exuberance and want to have their tats removed - a difficult process.) Then there are the celebrities who value glamour and adorn themselves with jewels and gaudy clothes, hoping that people will be distracted and won't notice they are superficial, inauthentic shells. Most of the celebrities I have met have no solid inner core.

There are also people who shun ornamentation. They understand that what is inside of them is what counts. You have already seen both types in action, Dylan. High school is great stage, as you know. So, continue to be real to yourself and others. Continue to be authentic and original. Continue to appreciate inner beauty in others. And keep developing the real you which lies within.

• Granny and I watched a super documentary a couple of nights ago. You would really appreciate it. The title is "Howard Zinn: You Can't be Neutral on a Moving Train." It's the title of one of his books - which we have. I hope someday you can read his books. He is one of my heroes. You can order the documentary through Netflix.

• In my world, creativity has two faces. One is the detail-oriented, often plodding, step-by-step, analytical, objective process. It usually falls under the scientific approach category. The other face is a messy process, full of hits and misses. It has no script, is generally ad-libbed, a creating-on-the-run sort of venture with a lot of adding and subtracting. Both approaches have their place. Not being a scientist and since I'm right-brained, I pursue the second approach. There is excitement in either approach. The world needs people who follow their creative instincts. Be one of those folks, Dylan.

• One of your strong points, Dylan, is that you care. Keep it up. Care about people, about your country, about this planet. Care about justice, freedom, about those whose needs are the greatest. In my lifetime, I believe our nation's leaders have created a society that favors some of us. I hope your generation will create one that cares about everyone.

• Common sense is not just common, it's also over-rated. Everyone has some common sense; that's why it's common. Relatively few people have uncommon sense, which is the ability to see what others see, but in a different, creative way. Uncommon sense is a critical element in wisdom.

A wise person develops uncommon sense then uses it. In today's vocabulary, uncommon sense is seeing things that are outside of the box. Develop your uncommon sense, Dylan. Develop the habit of looking at things differently.

Try to see what others don't. Sometimes you will accept conventional truths, but also try to look beyond (or under) those common, conventional beliefs, ideas or truths. It's okay to see what others see, but the trick is to go beyond - even to dream.

Granddaddyisms for a teenager

• When I was younger than you I spent some precious Saturday mornings at the William Nelson Gallery in Kansas City. My mother thought I should gain an appreciation of art. I was, to say the least, a reluctant participant. I would have strongly preferred to have been out playing with my friends. I was also exposed to the KC Symphony concerts to gain an appreciation of symphonic music and to museums to see antiquities and "old stuff." I'm sure I feigned disinterest and was likely vocal on expressing my antipathy toward these intrusions on my weekend play-time. But, as my mother clearly intended, over time I developed an appreciation of good art, good music and our culture. For most of my adult years, I have attended symphonic concerts and been a frequent visitor to art galleries and museums. We have, as you know, a sizable collection of art in our home.

The point of this, Dylan, is to urge you to develop an interest in the arts and in studying the culture of which you are a part. Seek out galleries and museums when you travel. Attend a symphonic concert and see how you like it. Whatever effort you make will make your old Granddad very, very happy.

• A cynical professor friend of mine once described college faculty as people who can easily dismantle temples but are incapable of building outhouses. Being a former academic, I must, in good faith, challenge my old friend's characterization. But his point is worth noting. It is easy to criticize and tear things down; tougher to create and build. Be a creator, Dylan.

• Live as if the world is watching you and you may become the unhappiest person on the funny farm.

• When someone disagrees with you, don't feel that you must immediately revise what you said. To do so may be a sign of insecurity. You may be agreeing because you want the person to like you. And if the other person wants you to agree with him, it may be a sign of his insecurity. Speak your piece, let the chips fall, and then later assess your feelings about the communication.

• Sometime in the future I hope you will take the time to study the work of a few of the better theologians. Next time we are together, ask me for some recommendations. I'll be happy to provide you a few names and share with you several of their publications.

But, until then, here is a statement from one of my favorites, Reinhold

Niebuhr:

"Nothing that is worth doing can be achieved in our lifetime; therefore we must be saved by hope. Nothing which is true or beautiful or good makes complete sense in any immediate context of history; therefore we must be saved by faith. Nothing we do, however virtuous, can be accomplished alone; therefore we must be saved by love."

Hold onto this one, Dylan. It's a keeper!

Meaning of life

As faithful readers know, during his teenage years I often communicated with Dylan, our oldest grandson, through Granddaddyisms. I have shared some of those with you.

When he was a senior at Iowa State University, he wrote a paper titled, "Why I am not going to change the world." It was his response to a friend's question. It was a very thoughtful and impressive document.

I thought you might be interested in my response to him:

Well done, Dylan. I especially liked the closing paragraph: "I am who I am today because of those around me. I am not going to change the world because that is not my goal. I am going to help to make the lives and ecosphere about me better, as others will help me and improve our environment. We will make the community better, and communities will make the world better. But, I alone am not going to change the world."

I understand your perspective that you, alone, will not change the world. But you will not be alone. You, and many others, have been changing the world and will continue to do so.

I believe we human beings exist to do exactly that. But we will likely do it with small acts of kindness and quiet, unheralded deeds that bring about positive changes in the lives of others. The effect each of us has in making our little part of the world better is far more likely to change the world than waiting for a big breakthrough.

I believe each of us should be judged not by the duration of our lives, but by the donation we make to the lives of others. Far too many individuals choose to live lives of self-gratification. In my opinion, they have wasted their lives. I believe a "good life" is one that is lived for others. But no one can live this type of life alone. To achieve it we must reach out to others for their assistance.

You have already learned this lesson. Your work in Tanzania and Uganda teaching in their schools, helping farmers cultivate their fields, conducting research that improved the lives of village workers, assisting with surgeries and delivering a child taught you invaluable lessons. Through your interactions with others, you have impacted the lives of many and brought about significant positive change in communities. I have no doubt you will continue to do so.

And in the process, you have learned that humanity is interconnected; that we are all brothers and sisters, and must make an effort to rid society of the rampant distrust of those who are "different" from us.

You have also learned the lesson that life must have a purpose bigger than ourselves and that each of us can make a significant difference in the lives of others. You have impacted lives, Dylan, and I have no doubt that you will continue to do so.

I am so very proud to be your granddad.

My hope is that you, and other people like you, will do a far better job than my generation in making the world a better and safer place for those yet unborn. While my generation has been concerned to some extent with changing the world, I suspect your generation will likely be more committed to "saving" the world.

What we haven't accomplished, you must or our planet will soon become irreversibly damaged.

One final thought: It is possible, Dylan, that the subject of changing (and saving) the world has a great deal to do with the meaning of life. What a heavy-and relevant-topic for all of us who care about this magnificent rolling ball and the people who inhabit it.

To err is human

• Dylan, be cautious in trusting a person who makes a strong declarative statement without attaching any reservations, qualifications or conditions.

• Back in the early 60s when I was active in the civil rights movement, I began a friendship with the minister, William Sloane Coffin. We corresponded before and during our family's 1964 summer in Alabama when I taught at Tuskegee Institute. Anyhow, in one of his books he discussed intolerance and wrote these words about people who engage in what psychiatrists call premature closure. "They are those who prefer certainty to truth, those in church who put the purity of dogma ahead of the integrity of love. And what a distortion of the Gospel it is to have limited sympathies and unlimited certainties, when the very reverse-to have limited certainties and unlimited sympathies - is not only more tolerant but far more Christian." A major part of my belief system is captured in this statement, which he has expressed far better than I could.

• People who insist they are RIGHT may not be fully human. To err is human.

• To know that you know little is a sign of intelligence. To communicate to others that you know little will likely win the respect of others who also recognize they know little. Those who communicate in this manner are often educated people.

• Dylan, I was very fortunate in my early adult years to discover that a defining priority in my life would be to try to make a positive difference in the lives of people, especially youngsters. One of the most meaningful experiences your granny and I ever had occurred when I was in graduate school at Colorado University when we together taught a Sunday school class for high school students. We began when they graduated from middle school and continued with the same 12 students until they graduated from high school. This experience was not only personally gratifying but necessary for my mental/emotional health. I came to understand that my life would be meaningless if I was not engaged in serving others. I also began to understand how extraordinarily fortunate I was to live with a person who, in her early years, also embraced this life goal as her own. There is no doubt in my mind that you are going to live a life of service to others, Dylan. If and/or when you begin looking for a mate, I suggest you give priority to someone who has similar life goals. I hope you will as lucky as I have been.

• If you ever find yourself doing something you shouldn't be doing or heading down a road that is going nowhere, have the good sense or courage to turn around. It's not strength of character that impels you to continue, but stubbornness. Inattentiveness or a bad choice may have put you on the wrong path and to continue only makes you obstinate and, possibly, a fool.

• Here is my best counsel for coping with life: look for the funny and learn to laugh.

Making a life

Self-knowledge leads to self-improvement which leads to self-fulfillment. I don't know any shortcuts.

Dylan, in your life you will face many challenges. Here are two of the most important ones: To make a living and to make a life. The latter is far more important than the former. If you choose to have a family, then you must confront the enormous challenge of striking a balance in your life between job, self-development including service to others, and family. It's hard for me to imagine anything more difficult and challenging than obtaining harmony between these three priorities. And what you will discover is that the challenge is ongoing. If you continually strive to achieve an equilibrium with these three critical aspects of your life, you will likely experience success and happiness. If you neglect to pay attention to any one of these three, you will likely experience problems and unhappiness.

• Think of time as a possession. You can lose everything except it. Learn to use it as an invaluable tool and an invaluable ally.

• I believe moral courage should be far more admired than physical courage. Moral cowardice reveals more about the depths of a person's spirit and personality than physical cowardice.

• I have no doubt that a major goal of yours is to lead a good life. My experience persuades me that a good life is the result of wise choices based on generous portions of good taste, judicious insights into your self-knowledge and experience, along with a burning desire to be a good person who tries to live honorably. A pinch of luck doesn't hurt either.

• Dylan, be wary of individuals who speak in superlatives because they show questionable judgment. Since exaggeration is a form of dishonesty, you must be cautious in accepting their communications.

• One of the most important lessons I learned when I was a young tournament tennis player was that great ability wasn't enough. I competed against a number of players who possessed more ability than me, yet I would often beat them. Why? Because they lacked dedication. They didn't practice with a commitment to excellence. They didn't use their gift. So, the lesson is that great ability without dedicated application equals a wasted talent. A commitment to hard work (practice) greatly enhances even a mediocre talent. Work hard and the benefits will surely follow.

• If you truly wish to enjoy people and have them appreciate you, then look for the good in them and pay minimal attention to their flaws. Your best friends will likely be those individuals who treat you similarly.

• Laughter, irony and paradox. Where would we humans be, Dylan, if we didn't have the capacity to deal with these?

Great achievements

*Thank you for your thoughtfulness in calling us to share the news that you have been accepted as a student at Iowa State University. You should be proud that you received early designation. Congratulations. It enables you to relax a bit and know you have a viable future, especially in a major that holds out such excitement and challenge, not to mention the probability of world travel and service. I find it difficult to imagine another college program that will rival this one.

But I assume you realize that that this doesn't mean you can put your senior year on cruise control. While some pressure is diminished, you surely are aware that what you do this year still counts. Dog it and you'll suffer consequences. Play it cool and you may find yourself out in the cold. No, what you do this year in school is critical with regard to your college years and to your life. So, resolve anew to give your senior year your best shot.

*Dylan, when you complete your formal education experience and there is no more degrees you wish to pursue, then I hope you will have learned two very important lessons. You realize how little you know, and you have learned the value off doubt.

*Some folks take a problem and make it more complex. Others take the same problem and simplify it. The second choice saves a lot of time.

*Ignorance and certainty are frequently linked. Certainty comes easily and stealthily to the person who is ignorant of his ignorance. Certainty often carries with it the baggage of arrogance.

*Dylan, in thinking about who you are and who you wish to become, may I suggest that you visit your passion. What do you really care about? The best individuals I have ever known carry with them a passion about life and within that context, a passion for certain values. What do you value? Conversely, you should be wary of people who exhibit no passion in their lives or in their interactions with others. These people are indifferent toward the conditions that direct or surround their lives or are under such rigid control that their emotions have atrophied. Some fear that exposing their emotions undermines their self-image. No matter the reason, they are basically unhappy, unfulfilled individuals. No one enjoys being around them. So, live with passion, Dylan. It's more fun. And you'll never lack for friends. People are drawn to those who exhibit passion.

*One of the great lessons in life is to understand that great achievements usually involve great risk. You have got to put yourself out there. And sometimes you won't know where it will lead. What you need to understand is that sometimes playing it safe is okay and sometimes it isn't. There will be times in your life when you will decide to "go for it." My own criteria is that if "safe" is dull, then I have a tendency to challenge myself and "go for it."

    *One of the significant challenges in life is to learn to distinguish the difference between theories, beliefs, opinions and facts.

Good luck!

A well-tended garden

• Dylan, look for ways (like going to Uganda) to increase the excitement in your life. The opportunities are there, if you want them to be. And by the way, excitement is closely related to passion.

• One of life's greatest challenges-and greatest achievements-is to gain control over yourself.

• One sign of mental health is when you take responsibility for yourself and stop projecting your problems onto others. It's the "I-blame-you" approach. "I blame you for my problems, my unhappiness, my lack of ability." A mentally healthy individual understands that he or she is responsible for the quality of his or her life.

• Have you discovered, Dylan, that there is high correlation between incompetence and laziness?

• Orderliness requires habits. Routines give rise to habits. The larger the organization, the more routines are encouraged, the more habits are rewarded, the more orderliness is worshiped. This is another reason why creative people are seldom tolerated and rarely happy in large organizations. There are exceptions to this principle, especially in Silicon Valley and other high tech locations.

• I have no doubt, Dylan, that you will have many good friends in your life. But I want you to understand that true friends are the individuals who will care enough about you to risk their friendship with you. Blessed are you if you have a few friends who will tell you things you may not wish to hear but need to hear. And blessed are your friends if you are that kind of person to them.

• Patience is a virtue unless you are a victim. Minorities (like African Americans) have rarely appreciated the concepts of "gradually" or "eventually" or "slowly."

• Be careful about committing yourself to do something for someone. When you give your word to a person you are honor-bound to keep it. When you tell a person you will do something, you have no choice but to do it. If you don't you have likely lost their respect and faith in you.

• Sadly, I fear the majority of people are easily deceived by appearances and image. We are raising a generation of uncritical spectators. Exterior perceptions have preference over inner realities. Be an original, Grandson.

• I believe, Dylan, there should be within each of us a well-tended garden in which revisions can grow. It should be a place where first impressions are modified, judgments are altered, opinions are discarded, truths are invalidated, beliefs are suspended and where we simply feel free to change our minds.

Only as far as I seek can I go

• I regret to tell you that no matter how sweet and kind we humans appear on the surface of our lives, each of us carries within us some venom. Controlling it is a lifetime challenge. It has the potential to harm not only our selves but others. Each of us is responsible for containing the poison within. We must discover how best to develop and use a personal enema to purge ourselves of it so that love and kindness can emerge and envelope our lives.

• Never be a whiner, Dylan. People who complain long and loud will discover they will soon lack for friends. When folks complain repeatedly about injustices committed against them you can be assured that their future will be filled with more.

Karin Ravin wrote this:
Only as high as I reach can I grow,
Only as far as I seek can I go,
Only as deep as I look can I see,
Only as much as I dream can I be.

• In adolescence some young people decide they know all they need to know to live a successful life. Nonsense! It's what one learns after they "know it all" that really counts. College is a great awakening for those who have become comfortable with who they are and what they know. A year or so ago you wrote that you didn't see why you needed a college education and why you just couldn't keep working in the parts store. I don't know if you still feel that way, but I certainly hope you don't. But if there is still any of that short-sided flapdoodle in you, get rid of it. NOW! Your life is ahead of you, and what you learn in the next four years will significantly determine who you become and what you will do with your life. So, a suggestion: buckle down a little harder on your studies for the rest of the year. Work at developing better study habits. Stop procrastinating. When you sit down to study, concentrate. Turn off the music. The study habits you leave high school with will likely be those you carry forth to college. They better be good ones or you will be in for a rude, harsh awakening.

• Sometimes in your life, you are going to lose. It's inevitable. Here's the trick: When you lose, don't lose the lesson. There is always one involved. Pay attention to the lesson.

• Here is another lesson: try to understand that not getting what you want is sometimes a wonderful stroke of luck.

• Dylan, someday you may be hired by an organization. Here is a particular point of view--not shared by all, by any means-that you may find helpful. You have, no doubt, learned that "rules are rules." No matter what you do or where you go, there will be rules. So, learn the rules so you know which ones make sense and how to break the stupid ones properly. You won't win arguments by explaining to someone who worships rules and procedures that you didn't know what they were or that no one told you, or whatever.

Excuses won't cut it. So, learn what they are and then figure out which ones are considered by those in power to be God-given, and which ones can be ignored or broken quietly. My experience, Dylan, is that within an organization, that has a lot of rules and regulations there will be a good number of bureaucrats. These are people whose motto is "No Exceptions!" You will need to learn how to deal with them.

Wonder, imagination and dreams

• Dylan, it's clear to me you are living a good, honorable life. There are two reasons why this is important. First of all, you can enjoy life now and not be filled with apprehension or worry about dire consequences of stupid actions and decisions. The other benefit is that later in life as you look back on these adolescent years, you can enjoy them again. You won't really appreciate this reality for another several decades, but you will. I promise.

• When someone says to you, "Let me be frank," or "Let me be honest with you," get your guard up and put your trust level at a low level. In my experience, honest people don't have to tell you.

• Outside of family, you can only be loved, Dylan, when you risk initiating the relationship.

• You need to develop a strategy for coping with change. Here are a few thoughts that might get you started: revere ritual, but feel free to revise; fight atrophy, but feel free to age; enjoy sunsets, but rejoice with sunrises. Mellow forward gently, adapting to new realities while holding fast to treasured memories.

• I have no doubt, Dylan, that you are going to be successful in life. Your underpinnings are solid and substantial. One way of measuring success is by determining what you have to give up in order to get it. However, there is also the matter of defining just what success is. We live in a society where far too many people equate success with the accumulation of money and possessions. I believe there is a better measure: to equate success with how valuable you are to society. You are valuable when you serve others selflessly and make a positive difference in their lives. You are valuable when you show compassion for others, especially those who are suffering or hungry or are victims of injustice. You are valuable when you confront the social structures that cause poverty, suffering and injustice. You are valuable when you stand up and speak out against practices and policies that favor the rich and powerful and deny equal treatment to those who are not.

• Try to understand, Dylan, that no one can make you angry without your consent, but you can be happy without another person's aid.

• Learning from your mistakes without dwelling on them is one of the toughest things to learn. Our capacity for self-flagellation is considerable.

• The best books you will ever read will be those that hold up a mirror before you.

• I believe each of us owe a debt to those who have given us a better, more civilized world to live in. I believe each of us should try to repay this debt by leaving it a bit better than we found it. If one chooses to have children, I hope they will be raised to feel this commitment.

• Of the many gifts you have been given, Dylan, I believe wonder, imagination and dreams are likely to be among the most treasured you will ever receive. I hope you will nurture each of them. Your life will be drab without these three gifts.

Effective leaders

When I hear about some of the things going on in your life, Dylan, I get the impression that you are becoming a leader. And I'm proud of you. But, listen up. In the long run of life, I want you to go way beyond being recognized as a leader. Let me explain.

Being of value to others and to society involves leadership. But, in my opinion, the world doesn't need more leaders. The world is filled with leaders and look at the condition of the world! The worst leaders are found in the capitols of nations because that is where the power is. And power attracts the corruptible. I am disenchanted with, and wary of, politicians. To me a politician is a person who believes that self-interest and/or party interests and/or special interests trump the public interest.

I want you to become an effective leader. Effective leaders serve the public interest. They are public servants. In government, we have far too many politicians and way too few public servants. While I have little respect for politicians, they are not entirely to blame for what they do or why they do it. The system of government is part of the problem. I agree with Winston Churchill who said that the United States has the worst government in the world, except for all the others.

But the concept of effective leaders goes far beyond politics. There are effective leaders in all aspects of life. They are the individuals who try to be of assistance to those in need, and who possess the skills and personal qualities that encourages people to respect and trust them. People follow them because they trust them to serve their best interests.

In my world, Dylan, there are three levels of leaders. At the lowest level are leaders. It's easy to become a leader. You can win a contest, get elected, get promoted, inherent the position, luck into it, or even walk down the street, turn around, notice someone is following you and decide, "Ah, I'm a leader." Leaders are a "dime-a-dozen."

Effective leaders are individuals who try to make a positive difference in the lives of others. They truly care about people and have compassion for them. They engage in selfless service as opposed to self-serving approaches. They believe that power is to be shared; it is never a "power over" approach. Their goal is to empower followers.

There is one level beyond this and they are the servant leaders. The best way to explain the difference between effective leaders and servant leaders is to say that the former are a work in progress; the latter simply are! SLs are servants first and leaders second. They lead by virtue of who they are and what they do and how they do it. People look up to them and listen to them and follow them because they "know" they have their best interests at heart. They are special individuals and the world has far too few of them.

My hope for you, Dylan, is that you strive to become an effective leader. These are the people who help others, who serve in ways that inspire them to become better than they believe they can be and do more in service to others than they believe they can do. They help us understand that ordinary people can serve others in extraordinary ways. So far, in your life, you are having the kind of experiences that are leading you to become an effective leader. I know you can become a special individual and perhaps in time, even a servant leader. It's in your hands. Remember, I'm always in your corner!

Real self-confidence

• I'm glad you are becoming more confident in what you are learning and doing. Real self-confidence is knowing that if you want to send the best, YOU go!

• You know what's critical about your formal education? It's understanding what is important after you have forgotten the facts. It's like the American history course you took several years ago. Remember my helping you learn dates and places? You're unlikely to remember that stuff. But what you ought to remember are the issues. Unfortunately, school history books do a poor job of illuminating issues, which are controversial or reflect poorly on our nation's leaders. The books have been sanitized! There is a study out on this, which became a book. It's called "Lies My Teacher Told Me." That is a lousy title because it is not the teachers' fault. Citizens who select or approve school textbooks do not want young people to know the true history of our country. How white people treated Native Americans or Black people, for instance. So there is a "heroification" of leaders. The textbook companies know public officials and school boards won't buy texts that tell the truth about our nation's history so they produce homogenized versions. There is only one history textbook I recommend you read and it's "A People's History of the United States" by Howard Zinn. It is the only history book I know of that deals honestly with our country's past.

• I'm pleased you are reading the chapter on "Change" in my book. Here is a little something I didn't put in it: Many people will change when they feel the heat, not when they see the light.

• Back when I was your age, I really didn't know what adolescent rebellion was. I was too happy and content to live in a home (most of my friends were crowded together in small apartments) and I knew I should be grateful for what we had. I didn't have many clothes, but what I had I took care of because I knew my parents couldn't afford to buy me new ones. So I hung them up in my small closet when I took them off and was careful to ask my Mom to patch them or sew pieces together when they split. So, what I'm wondering is whether you feel the need to continue your little rebellion by tossing your good clothes onto the floor or whether it's time to begin hanging them up and taking care of them? I really doubt you will leave them wherever they fall when you share a room next year at college with a roommate. This might be a good time to make a move into adulthood. What do you think?

• No, I'm not crazy about politicians either. For a politician to possess a little bit of power is like a person having a little bit of pregnancy. It's there, and it's going to get bigger!

• How often we ascribe to strangers or acquaintances power and strength, which, in truth, they do not possess. Once we establish relationships with these same individuals, we quietly strip them of these qualities, recognizing that they are, indeed, fallible human beings, like us. We do it with teachers, for instance, and you will likely do it next year with your professors, Dylan. It's okay, but just remember, they have flaws just like the rest of us.

• No, I don't believe some people have charisma. I believe we invest them with it. Once you get to know a person-really know them-the charisma disappears. Then they become just as human and flawed as the rest of us.

Self-deception is a matter of degree

* Pre-occupation with the past makes us sitting ducks for the future and prevents us from fully appreciating the present. Pre-occupation with the future indicates we are probably underestimating the lessons of the past while diminishing our chances of savoring the present.

* Phrases like "I deserved that," or "I had it coming," indicate in our minds that retribution for whatever misdeed we committed is likely appropriate. It also reveals that within the person is a sense of justice that acknowledges the difference between right and wrong.

* Self-deception is a matter of degree.

* Be wary, Dylan, of people who say their actions are not really under their control. Whether God is directing the person, or Satan, or a crazed dictator, or the forces of nature, their intent is to absolve themselves of responsibility for their behavior and justify whatever they do in the righteousness of obedience.

* Dylan, expect reason to be true to itself, not to you, and you will have taken a major step toward wisdom.

* The "What's-in-it-for-me" attitude is certain to culminate in adult whiners and persistent sufferers whenever their hours or days or weeks fall short of producing the kind of happiness they think they deserve. The consequence for family friends and colleagues who hold different values will be staggering. How will these bogus victims relate to legitimate victims, for instance?

What will be their understanding of compassion? How often will we hear them cry out, "It isn't fair!" How will they handle defeats? What quality of life will they likely have?

* Philosopher Immanuel Kant argued that human beings should seek not to be happy, but to be deserving of happiness. Happiness was a consequence of a life well-lived. I wonder how this idea would catch on with young people your age, Dylan?

* I suspect that those who believe they are entitled to happiness are morally estranged and spiritually isolated. I also suspect they will spend their lives seeking personal prestige, material success, instant gratification, the accumulation of power, financial security and continual entertainment-goals that define their concept of happiness.

* I believe that courtesy, manners and civility are the three pillars of a cultured person. What do you think, Dylan?

Final words

Yes, Dylan, there were "Big Boys" in my high school way back in the early 40s. Just like now, they are boys who believe aggression validates their "manhood." They try hard to impersonate their concept of real men, believing that macho, combative behavior is a sign of strength. They are the bullies of the world.

Big Boys are insensitive to recognizing, much less appreciating, the strengths of others that they do not possess-gentleness, tenderness, softness, compassion, vulnerability and sensitivity, for instance.

Those who believe aggression validates their manhood have an undeveloped concept of the heroic. True heroism includes examining one's need to be aggressive and expanding one's self-awareness.

Imposing one's power upon another is an indication of arrogance, not of courage or masculinity.

Big Boys are on the way to becoming men when they learn respect for those who are actively engaged in preventing violence and no longer revere those who seek violent engagements. They are on the way to becoming men when they appreciate Gandhi's statement: "Non-violence and cowardice go ill together." I can imagine a fully armed man to be at heart a coward. But true non-violence is an impossibility without courage.

Those who attribute to themselves imaginary superior qualities of character and to others inferior qualities are morally challenged individuals. Association with them is risky; the slightest perceived affront will likely cause them to turn on you.

But when dealing with Big Boys you need to understand that often their mean-spiritedness is because they have so little in their life to look back on with pride and so little to look forward to with hope. Many of them express anger at successful people as a way of getting even with them.

Dylan, this is my final Granddaddyism. You will soon be entering the University and will have enough challenges without concerning yourself with my musings.

So, a couple of final thoughts.

There is much negativism in the "Big Boys" segment above and that is not how I want to end this series of Granddaddyisms. So, let me close this series on a more positive note.

You will never find an individual whose behavior and ideals are exactly like yours. So, be slow to anger and quick to understand.

Each of us is an imperfect individual living in an imperfect world. We face the constant struggle of respecting those whose behavior and ideals are different from ours. I believe we are called to respect individuals not because of their behavior but because of their humanity and personal value.

In other words, you need not like everyone you meet, but you can try to love and respect individuals for whom you feel a distinct aversion.

The very best of human relationships develops when we really care about one another and have genuine concern for their well-being.

To live a life of meaning and enjoy relationships with others, it is critical that we remind ourselves of our common humanity and our common need for redemption.

You are a good person, Dylan. I am confident you will lead a good life.

You have my respect and my love.

A grandson replies

By DYLAN CLARK

Editor's note – The following is a self-explained substitute this week for Ron Barnes' regular newspaper column.

If you have been a Daily Courier reader over the past few decades, you may have come to know Ron Barnes through his weekly columns. Readers may too know Ron by his dedication and contributions to the Prescott community. I, however, know Ron simply as Granddaddy.

Nine years ago, during my late teenage years, Ron began sending me letters once a week. His words documented lessons he had absorbed from his and others' successes, mistakes he made, and 80 years of accumulated wisdom. These lessons became known as "Granddaddyisms." Over the past few years, Ron has shared many of these insights with you, too.

A few weeks ago, I asked my Granddaddy (who asked the editor) if I could write a column for the Courier. I felt it only fair that, after years of him writing about me, I had a chance to respond at least once! More importantly, I wanted to share what these Granddaddyisms have meant to me.

Over the last week, I have reread many of the original letters from him, each stirring memories of where I was when I first read them nearly a decade ago. As I passed over the documents, some gave me pause as I remember being irritated by their implications (in one, Ron tells me to clean my room), while on other pages I discovered the origin of anecdotes that I have held onto nearly word for word. And, while my 18-year-old self never consciously considered the complete meaning/significance of these years' worth of letters, I feel my takeaways then and now are the same.

Interwoven throughout the counsel that Ron has shared with us is a deep appreciation for learning. Ron has always been an educator and a student. As a child, I often struggled to see the importance of education, making this characteristic of Ron's feel like a dividing line between grandparent and grandchild. During my elementary and junior high years, I did well in subjects like geography and science, but as a child under the dyslexic umbrella, reading and writing coursework was a battle for me. Although I have become better at reading over the past decade, with the help of incredible teachers, my parents, and assistance from Brain Integration sessions, the most important growth has been a newfound appreciation for education, after childhood misconceptions of learning as simply sitting behind a desk.

In sharing his Granddaddyisms with us, Ron was doing what he has done his entire life: empowering others to learn about themselves and the world around them. Ron has taught me to seek out new perspectives, to be awed and inspired by the depths of human knowledge, and to ask nuanced questions and demand complex answers. Ron has lived by his value in education. I can only assume that is why he felt it was so important for him to spend a summer teaching at Tuskegee Institute during the 1960s — for him and his family to learn, for his students to etch new perspectives.

In October 2008, Ron told me "a college education is the best way I know to provide you with the skills necessary to face the future with confidence. You will be limiting yourself without it." I have been extraordinarily privileged to have had the opportunity to go to university, parents who made time to help me study, and dedicated teachers with their resources in their classrooms.

A final lesson that Ron has taught me is the importance of action. Ron and Betsy have never been the type to sit on the sidelines: they learn about issues, and then act with conviction. Whether it is addressing racial inequality or reducing hunger in the community or something else entirely, it is important to find an issue that does feed your passion; to spend time learning about that issue and listening to different perspectives on how to solve it, and then to act.

And, as I am sure Ron would agree, writing is one of the many powerful actions in our arsenal. He has shown us the power of words through his columns.

I will forever cherish the Granddaddyisms, and I hope you too have learned from them. To me the most powerful Granddaddyism, however, has not been explicitly published in the Courier. It is the narrative that Ron and Betsy have written over their 85 years of working to make their communities and world a better place.

Note from Ron: Dylan Clark graduated cum laude from Iowa State University with a double major in Environmental Studies and Global Resource Management, and received his Master's Degree from McGill University in Montreal, Canada, in Health Geography. He is now employed by McGill as a research assistant. His research focuses on the effects of global warming on Indigenous people.

Dylan and his partner Elise

WIT

Ron wearing his "Introverts have more fun" shirt

Four letter words

Learning certain words was part of growing up.

In elementary school, teachers decided which ones were acceptable and should be learned by us students.

But we learned pretty quickly that on the playground and in the neighborhood, there were a whole slew of exciting words that signaled some sort of maturity primarily because they were unacceptable to teachers and, more importantly, to our parents.

I'm referring, of course, to "swear words."

Frankly, most of us used them poorly because we really didn't know what they meant or when to use them. So, we sort of watched and waited, paying respectful attention to older kids who could roll them off their tongues with ease and conviction. We imitated them as best we could, knowing that someday we would catch on to their meaning and would be able to swear with flawless perfection.

High school provided rich opportunities to practice cuss-word skills so by the time I reached college in 1948, I was confident I had mastered enough words to hold my own against most anyone.

However, I had not reckoned with the experience and worldliness of the WW II veterans. I was clearly not in their league. So I listened and learned for a couple of years, biding my time until the veterans had graduated and I was a third-year student.

I was also captain of the tennis team. This was a fortuitous position to exert leadership and make up ground for two years of relative quiet on the cussing front. The tennis court became the home of the blue.

But not for long. After one heated emission with a special scatological reference, our coach took me aside and suggested I (and the rest of the team) find less provocative words that would permit us to blow off steam without being offensive to spectators. As team captain, I accepted the challenge.

Quickly I determined that four letter words were out. "So, how about a five-letter word," I said to myself. And in a rare moment of inspiration, I had it.

"Mercy!"

That was it. It caught on immediately. Tennis team members enthusiastically accepted it. Golfers shouted it through the hills and trees of the Williamsburg (Virginia) Inn golf course. A basketball player screamed it after missing a lay-up; the referee wisely declined to call a technical on him.

Opponents also took to it. "Mercy" was a lot more fun than their old, trusted and true four-letter words. Athletes and spectators alike inevitably smiled when they heard the word ring out from athletic venues.

But, for me, it really had only a one year life. At the beginning of my senior year, I had moved on to embrace a new four-letter word. Finally, a girl had come into my life and I began to place a high value on the word, LOVE. That girl and I still use it constantly.

Maturity also brought with it an appreciation of other four-letter words-like care, hope, soul, life, self, kind and wise.

These have become particular favorites along with one that seems to have fallen out of favor-duty.

I also wonder if the word "work" has the same meaning to the young as it had for my generation.

Anyhow, I seem to have lived a lifetime learning about and using four-letter words. I guess there is only one left to think about and I am in no hurry to do so. It begins and ends with "D."

Local attraction is magical, life-changing

When I was a young nipper, maybe five or six, my mother told me that she was going to take me to a magical place. That's all she said to me. But it was enough to persuade me to give up my usual Saturday morning frolic with friends in the nearby park.

We both bundled up, then she took my hand and we walked about a mile to a building I'd never seen before. It didn't look very special to me, but when we went inside, I gradually began to understand.

That place changed my life. It WAS magical. And I've been visiting buildings like it ever since.

What is it?

Well, for one thing, it's the most exciting place in Prescott. Ditto Prescott Valley and Chino Valley.

It's where the most learned people in the world debate and argue.

It's where ideas are discussed, where conflicts are started and sometimes resolved, where good and evil are put on display for all of us.

It's where gods and devils struggle in constant battle.

It's where the past is revered and the future explored.

It's where men's and women's lives are examined, where historical figures are scrutinized to see whether they measure up against the judgment of history.

It's where children can listen to stories that will change their lives. It's where the world's greatest storytellers wait for her. It's where a child can begin to satisfy her insatiable curiosity, where her wonder can be extended, provoked, stimulated.

It's an awesome place, almost beyond one's ability to comprehend.

It's an intimidating place. You could spend your lifetime there and only scratch the surface of what's available.

It's a classless place. Regardless of educational or socioeconomic level, it beckons you.

It's where you can explore the world, take trips, visit foreign lands and be home for dinner all in one day.

It's the most human place around. It's where endeavor, human aspiration, human agony, human ecstasy, human failures and human triumphs are laid out before you.

It's not a place for the faint of heart; it's terribly exciting and even frightening all at once.

It's also a dangerous place. There are ideas, values, theories, principles and beliefs there that are downright scary, radical, heretical, perverse and subversive. Some people don't want others to explore what's there for fear they may learn about ideas that will change the way they think or question their beliefs or faith.

It's where arrogance and certitude and prejudice are challenged. It's where our limitations become evident.

It's where the best and worst of our lives collide.

It's where adventure is king, where journeys are begun, where one's vision is expanded.

It's where the human spirit can be renewed, idealism rekindled, and our lives re-created.

It's where our basic freedoms are preserved. It's the most tolerant historical institution in society.

It's the one permanent oasis in our community. It's where one can sit quietly, uninterrupted, to ponder, reflect, contemplate and be introspective.

It's our public library. And today begins National Library Week.

So, this week, when you go to the library, pause and give thanks that it exists. As for me, I shall carry my gratefulness one step further. I shall hug a librarian. Don't get yourself into a snit folks. I live with a former librarian.

Father's travails begin on day one

There are a great many experiences that are sorely underrated. Becoming a father is one of them.

At least for me. If it weren't, I wouldn't frequently recall - all too vividly - every single step of this incredible adventure, nor would I wake up in a cold sweat from the dream that plays each May.

Here is what happened.

I remember escorting my wife to the hospital on that historical day in Boulder, Colorado. I have no doubt that I walked in there with my chest seriously puffed out thinking to myself that no man could ever look or feel as powerful as I felt at that moment.

I mean, look what I did! For there, waddling next to me was my wife verifying my conviction, with her stomach covering everything except her face and lower legs. Yep, that's power when you make your spouse look like that!

As soon as they wheeled My Beloved into the delivery room, I met the challenge the way any strong, macho, virile (obviously virile) male meets it. I threw up!

In fact, I understand I'm still on record in this particular hospital as being the only father to have his own room when his wife was giving birth. And after WE brought forth our daughter, I'll never forget what happened: The doctor came in to see me.

He asked, with a barely concealed smirk on his face, "Are you and your wife thinking about having another child?"

"Yes sir."

"Then perhaps we might chat about how you might prepare next time."

He didn't say word one to her; she did just great. But I was sick as a dog.

However, good puppy that I am, I learned. So, two years later in the middle of the night when she gave me the elbow and whispered it was time to go to the hospital, I jumped right out of bed and went into our own bathroom and threw up.

"Well, at least you're not going to embarrass me the way you did last time we went through this," she uttered."

"Don't count on it," I replied. "I don't think I'm through yet!"

And I wasn't.

Then, when we arrived at the hospital, with my luck wouldn't you know that the same nurse was on duty who was there before.

"Oh, hello," she said to me much too sweetly, "Please follow me. I'm sure we can find an empty room for you."

No sireee, people just don't understand what we fathers go through.

Happy Father's Day to all of us stalwart, valiant men.

Do you remember?

This one is for all of you "old timers" out there.

If you were a youngster during the '30s and early '40s, you likely have some precious memories that probably include a degree of nostalgia and romance, along with tough times.

So here are some of mine that may provoke you to recollect some of yours.

I remember:

... writing "Kilroy was here" on the sides of freight cars and wondering who Kilroy was.

... seeing a pregnant woman and asking my friend how she got that way; he didn't know either.

... haircuts for 25 cents and the bright red tonic the barber put on my hair when he finished.

... desk ink wells and the tempting curls of the little girl in the seat in front of me.

... doing it on the dare of a friend and listening to her screams and watching her hair drip.

... being suspended from school for a day and having to drink some castor oil.

... chocolate sodas thick enough to be eaten with a spoon.

... large cuffs on my blue jeans and metal buttons instead of zippers. The buttons were undependable.

... wondering why girls always giggled when I walked by.

... Burma Shave signs on country highways, and thinking that someday I wanted to write good poetry like that.

... paying 10 cents to ride a pony led by a bored old man.

... seeing my first television in the experimental room of the Kansas City Power & Light building and thinking it would never replace movies.

... listening to Jack Armstrong, The Shadow Knows, One Man's Family, and Fibber McGee and Molly.

... being told that iodine wouldn't hurt, but it always did.

... getting my first pair of knickers and feeling quite grown-up.

... an old swimming hole where we stripped and swam until girls discovered it. I never went back after that.

... looking through old National Geographic magazines for those pictures.

... getting my Jack Armstrong ring de-coder through the mail so I could help the war effort by catching spies.

... standing on the top of the apartment building with my buddies scanning the sky for German airplanes.

... sugar rationing and meat rationing and asking my mother when we got our first ration books if we still had to pay for food.

... collecting newspapers and scrap metal for the school war bond drive.

... going to double and triple feature picture shows and wondering why anyone would go to a theater that only showed one movie.

... getting a sty the first time I took a girl to a movie and deciding I'd never go out on a date again.

Say it today, regret it tomorrow

Have you ever said something then immediately wished you hadn't?

If you answered "No" I suspect you either have a lousy memory or a very selective one.

All of us have uttered things that have come back to haunt us.

"I can tell you for a fact she won't give us a test today."

"Honey, that red and orange blouse looks great on you. Now let's go. We're already late as it is!"

"Okay, okay, I love your broccoli, banana, avocado, black bean puree. I hope we have it every night this week!"

But mutterings like these are small potatoes compared to what some of our illustrious citizens have said.

Here are a few of the more memorable ones:

After turning down the role of Rhett Butler and hearing that Clark Gable had accepted it, Gary Cooper issued this statement: "Gone with the Wind is going to be the biggest flop in Hollywood history. I'm just glad it will be Clark Gable who's falling flat on his face and not Gary Cooper."

In urging President McKinley to abolish the U.S. Patent office in 1899, the Patent Office director used this argument: "Everything that can be invented has been invented."

Early in his career when he was a young writer with the Toronto Star, Ernest Hemingway received this appraisal from a fellow reporter: "You'll never get anywhere with those damned little short sentences."

Even noted historians get it wrong sometimes. After a long interview with Hitler in 1936, Arnold J. Toynbee said: "I am convinced of Hitler's sincerity in desiring peace in Europe."

"I think there's a world market for maybe five computers," said Thomas J. Watson, chairman of IBM in 1943.

Under the heading of wishful thinking come these words from movie producer Darryl F. Zanuck: "Video won't be able to hold onto any market it captures after the first six months. People will get tired of staring a plywood box every night."

Lee De Forest, inventor of the audio tube, said this in 1957: "Man will never reach the moon regardless of all future scientific advances." Guess what happened just 12 years later.

Jim Denny, booking agent for the Grand Ole Opry, gave this talent appraisal to a young man after his first performance: "You ain't goin' nowhere with that, son. You ought to go back to drivin' a truck." Elvis persevered anyhow.

In 1964 a United Artists studio executive rejected Ronald Reagan for the role of president in the movie "The Best Man" with these words: "Reagan doesn't have the presidential look."

And here is my personal favorite: "The world will little note nor long remember what we say here, but it can never forget what they did here." We do remember, Mr. Lincoln.

The receptacle

Fair warning! Some of you may choose not to read this column. It is not for the faint of heart. Or those who have queasy stomachs. Only the curious and mildly adventurous should proceed.

Let us narrow the scope. Faithful readers will recall that I lived in Kansas City, Missouri, during my early years. Those who lived in the KC area or visited that city back in the '30s or '40s no doubt remember a certain aroma that followed the wind and permeated vast areas of the twin communities on the Missouri and Kansas border.

I am referring to the Kansas City Stockyards.

In those days, the yards were a huge enterprise. Spreading over many acres, they were a formidable entity. On certain days, their presence manifested itself as far east as Independence, Missouri, and as far south as Shawnee Mission, Kansas.

Such was the influence of the livestock business that my particular elementary school-and others I later learned-took our once-a-year field trip to the huge Swift packing plant each spring. Once we diverted to the awesome Cudahy plant, but that hardly qualified as a new and different experience.

"What?" you may ask. "No field trips to the famous William Rockhill Nelson Art Gallery or the Swope Park Zoo, or the huge train station and yards, or the beautiful, impressive World War I Memorial, or ... ?" Nope. Just meat packing plants.

But, as Max Schulman used to write, "I digress!"

Narrowing further, the indelicate subject of this peroration is located in the large stockyards building that adjoined the yards. This is where the business of the stockyards took place. And it was in one of those many offices that my father worked as a bookkeeper.

It was on a Saturday morning when I was, maybe 5 or 6 years old, that I rode to work with my dad for the first time. This was a big adventure. He was taking me with him to meet his co-workers and see where he disappeared for five or six days each week. He also told me we would ride in an elevator. Imagine my excitement!

In "his" office I met the boss, Mr. Bauman, along with a half-dozen other men. "Why don't you walk around the building for a while, Butch. I'm going to be here for a couple of hours."

I thought this was a good idea, although what I really wanted to ask him was what are those shiny brass things beside everyone's desk? But he was busy talking with someone, so I decided to explore the building and see if there were more of those things in other offices.

71

There were! In every office and, it appeared to me, by every desk except those where women worked. I didn't have any idea what they were, but I did discover that some men didn't like them. They spat at them!

There you have it. Of course, Dad later told me what they were and what they were for. He said they were for men only. Which meant, I assumed, that women and children weren't to use them. That sounded okay to me because, frankly, I thought they were smelly and icky anyhow.

I saw a brass spittoon in one of Prescott's antique stores last week. It was all cleaned up and shiny. "Looks good," I thought to myself, "but I know its history."

I passed it by!

My first valentine

The first Valentine's Day I remember was when I was in the third grade.

The day began innocently enough.

I suppose many events of great import do.

And since the day started like any other, I had no inkling that anything special was in the air. Consequently, I thought nothing of it when the blonde-haired girl who joined our class several weeks earlier jumped into line in front of me when we marched back from recess.

As we entered the classroom, she turned and handed me a small red card with a heart on it.

The message was simple but awesome: "Be My Valentine."

This was an entirely new thought to me. No one had ever asked this of me before. I spent the rest of the morning wondering what obligations this would mean if I accepted.

Of course, it occurred to me that I could say no. However, she was a new classmate and something deep inside of me told me it would be rude to refuse her request.

So, at lunchtime as we opened our brown sacks and attacked our sandwiches, I looked over to the next aisle and nodded. She winked at me.

That was true second bewildering lesson of the day.

I didn't know what a wink meant, although since she also smiled I assumed it meant the agreement was sealed.

Had I known then what I know now, I would have understood and interpreted those consequential acts for what they were-entrapment and commitment.

Obviously, her experience at a big-time school had prepared her for conquests beyond my limited range of understanding. The ways and wiles of girls, especially aggressive ones, were far beyond my experience. No second grade psychologist had told me that girls developed faster than little boys and, thus, were prepared to enter into relationships that little boys could hardly comprehend.

Anyhow, during the afternoon recess, the contract was sealed. She grabbed my hand, yanked me over to the teeter-totter and began bouncing me up and down. I didn't know what love was, but I recall some vague thought that this might be it.

This disquieting feeling was reinforced when she later knocked the breath out of me with a well-placed soccer kick. I had never known a recess period like that. Being a Valentine was downright exciting!

73

Later that afternoon during art, all of us moved around to different desks. She sat in front of me, turned and smiled, and I dreamed of eternal togetherness. When she handed me a heart with an arrow in it that she had drawn, I knew whose heart had been pierced. Clearly this was a day unlike any other in the adventure called school.

In my rapturous state, I was sure that our relationship had advanced to some mysterious stage that called for a deeper commitment. Of course, I had no idea how to consummate it. But I was now aflame with desire to let her know that what we had was special.

Then the perfect expression of love came to me. Bobby Cox and Patty Conrad were a hot item in the second grade. They had been "going together" for a week now. I remembered how it started. My uncontaminated concept of the romantic told me that Bobby's dramatic ploy could succeed again.

Smiling confidently, I carefully grabbed a bunch of "my girl's" long curls and dipped them into my desk inkwell. Unaware of this loving beauty treatment, she changed position, enabling me to color more of her locks. I wiped them semi-dry and sat back pleased and proud.

Laughter violated my glorious moment and her subsequent cries when some sneak handed her a mirror shattered my reverie. Within a few minutes it became clear that our budding relationship was over. Her harsh looks at me let me know that my first experience as a Valentine was finished. It lasted less than a day.

I've since learned that chocolates or flowers are better gifts than ink.

But I've never forgotten "my first love."

And those magic words, "Be My Valentine!"

The will

There are a great many folks in the Prescott area thinking about the following topic. So this one is for you: a document I have kept for the last 50 years.

Every so often I pull it out to reread. You may find yourself doing the same thing.

A lawyer's last will:

I, Charles Lounsberry, being of sound and disposing mind and memory, do hereby make and publish this, my last will and testament, in order, as justly may be, to distribute my interest in the world among those succeeding me:

That part of my interest which is known in law and recognized in the sheep-bound volumes as my property, being inconsiderable and of no account, I make no distribution of this in my will. My right to live, being but a life estate, is not at my disposal, but these things accepted, all else in the world I now proceed to device and bequeath.

ITEM: I give to good fathers and mothers, in trust for their children, all good little words of praise and encouragement and all quaint pet names and endearments and I charge said parents to use them justly, but generously, as the needs of their children shall require.

ITEM: I leave to children inclusively but only for the term of their childhood, all and every flower of the field and blossoms of the woods, with the right to play among them freely, according to the customs of children, warning them at the same time about thistles and thorns. And I devise to children the banks of the brooks and the golden sands beneath the waters therein, and the white clouds that float high over the giant trees.

And I leave to children the long, long days to be merry in a thousand ways, and the night and the train of the Milky Way to wonder at, but subject, nevertheless, to the rights hereinafter given to lovers.

ITEM: I devise to boys, jointly, all the useful idle fields, all pleasant waters where one may swim, all snow clad hills where one may coast, all streams and ponds where one may fish, or where, when grim Winter comes, one may skate, to hold the same for the period of their boyhood, and all meadows with clover blossoms and butterflies, thereof; the woods with their appurtenances, the squirrels and birds, the echoes and strange noises and all distant places which may be visitant, together with the advantages there found. And I give to said boys, each his own place at the fireside at night, with all the pictures that may be seen in the burning wood, to enjoy without let or hindrance, and without encumbrance or care.

75

ITEM: To lovers I devise their imaginary world, with whatever they may need, as the stars of the sky, the red roses by the wall, the bloom of the hawthorn, the sweet strains of music and aught else that they may desire to figure to each other the lastingness and beauty of their love.

ITEM: To young men, jointly, I devise and bequeath all boisterous and inspiring sports of rivalry, and I give them the disdain of weakness and undaunted confidence in their own strength. Though they are rude, I leave them the power to make lasting friendships, and of possessing companions, and to them, exclusively, I give all merry songs and grave choruses to sing with lusty voices.

ITEM: To those who are no longer children or youths or lovers, I leave memory, and other poets, if there may be others, to the end that they may live the old days over again, freely and fully, without tithe or diminution.

ITEM: To our loved ones with snowy crowns, I bequeath the happiness of old age, the love and gratitude of their children, until they fall asleep.

Note: This strange will was left by a young lawyer who died some years ago in a ward for the insane in the almshouse of Cook County, Illinois. The will was found in his coat. On a resolution of the Chicago Bar Association, the document was sent to probate and was spread on the records of Cook County.

Sourpuss

I was sitting quietly in the Y lobby recently when an old sourpuss walked in and angrily dished out a string of loud criticisms to one of the ladies manning the reception desk.

When he completed his cranky oration, he walked to the coffee table, got himself a free cup, then sat down in a chair and turned his evil eye on a nearby group of high school youngsters who were enjoying themselves. They had the good sense to pay him scant attention.

I wondered if he is also one of the letter-writers who send such angry diatribes to the newspaper. Seems like we have more than our share of acerbic individuals in our beautiful community.

They walk around with tight, determined scowls. Their facial expressions and body movements declare, "Don't mess with me!"

I rarely do, although my innate and largely unrestrained perversity usually pushes me into smiling and I sometimes inquire, "How ya doin' today?"

Usually the only reply I receive is either a mumble or a suppressed gargle.

My favorite response was from a sour man who said, "I'm doing okay, but it won't last." Without another word, he walked on.

It wasn't a bad line, as responses go. But as a commentary on his view of the present and future, it demonstrated why he's so vinegary. Even when his day is going all right, he expects things to go bad.

There is no question in my mind he will be proven right.

His world is seen as a negative; pessimism is his adopted outlook.

It's a matter of perspective-it's how we look at things.

For instance, if I smile when I speak, you will likely return my smile with a friendly acknowledgement. He returns it with a bitter response.

If I ask you to move your shopping cart so I can push mine down the grocery aisle, you do so courteously. He calls me an impatient bleep.

To me, he is sour; to him, he is realistic.

Each of us tends to interpret the present to our benefit. We distort reality it so it fits into our perceived view of the world. We reinforce our attitudes, biases, prejudices, likes and dislikes by coloring what we see and hear so it coincides with what we already believe.

I am flexible, you are pigheaded.

I am fair; you are biased.

I am creative; you are a cliché.

You and I can provide two distinct interpretations when witnessing the

77

same event. Further, a double standard of behavior is a clear characteristic-I may judge you critically, but tend to evaluate myself kindly.

I remind myself of this perspective every time I see one of our sour citizens.

I tell myself it is only a temporary mask he is wearing, that as soon as he gets home and turns his attention to his favorite hobby, it will be replaced by a peaceful countenance.

But I don't really believe it.

He has allowed himself to become down on life and then blames others for his jaundiced attitude rather than accepting responsibility for permitting events in his life to have shaped his warped view.

Perspective!

Be careful with it-lest it grow sour on you.

Introverts and Extroverts

A number of you responded to my column on introversion in early October.

So, here's a sequel about the care and feeding of introverts, along with some of the major differences between introverts and extroverts.

If you are an extrovert you likely interact every day with an introvert and the chances are you are likely driving this person nuts. Introverts find extroverts very tiring. To an introvert, an hour or two with an extrovert is a wearing experience.

Extroverts assume that their company is always welcome. They have difficulty understanding why some people need to be alone. Most have little understanding of what it is like to be an introvert.

Introverts generally have to be dragged to parties and then need several days to recuperate. Extroverts jockey with one another to see who can be the life of the party.

Introverts are described as guarded, loners, self-contained, reserved, taciturn, private and narrow. Extroverts are seen as vibrant, warm, confident, empathic, outgoing, and big-hearted. They are often called "people persons."

Introverts are not necessarily shy or withdrawn individuals. But they do need hours alone every day. They love quiet conversations about feelings or ideas but seem awkward in groups and maladroit at small talk. After being socially "on" for an hour or two, introverts need to turn off for several hours to recharge. To be alone with their thoughts is as restorative as sleep.

Extroverts are overrepresented in public life. They seem to come fully to life around other people. Few introverts rise to the top in politics. One exception was Calvin Coolidge, the Yogi Berra of politics. Remember his statement? "Don't you know that four-fifths of all our troubles in this life would disappear if we would just sit down and keep still?" Then there's this one: "If you don't say anything, you won't be called on to repeat it."

From a recent article in The Wall Street Journal "The Introverted Entrepreneur," a case is made that introverts have unique skills that make them valuable in the business world, like the ability to focus for long periods of time, a propensity for balanced and critical thinking, a knack for quietly empowering others. Successful introverted business leaders include Warren Buffet, Bill Gates, Mark Zuckerberg and Marissa Mayer, CEO of Yahoo.

Susan Cain, author of "Quiet, The Power of Introverts in a World That Can't Stop Talking" says that introverts succeed because they create and

79

lead companies from a very focused place. "They steer clear of the cult of personality. Their emphasis is on creating something, not on themselves."

Introverts have this problem: they wait to speak until they have something to say. Not because they are shy, but because they are thinking and processing. In other words, introverts tend to think before talking; extroverts tend to think by talking.

The more extroverts in a meeting, the longer the meeting will last. Every introvert knows this for a fact. So the introverts will do whatever they can to a) avoid the gathering or b) become chairman so they can move the meeting along.

Contrary to what some extroverts believe, introverts can have good social skills. They are not necessarily morose or misanthropic. They love long conversations that explore intimate thoughts or passionate interests.

To an introvert "Hell is other people at breakfast." The motto of introverts is "I'm okay and you (extroverts) are okay in small doses." Their favorite response to talkative extroverts is to say, "I'm an introvert. You are a wonderful person and I like you. Now please shush."

Finally, when you extroverts see an introvert lost in thought, don't say "What is the matter?" or "Are you all right?" P.S. Don't say anything else either!

Laughter and life

When was the last time you met someone who was really different? You know, the kind of person who just stands out from the crowd. Well, I met him a few years ago.

He wore rose-colored glasses. I asked him why.

"Because," he replied, "I believe the world is out to do me good."

How's that for a definition of inverse paranoia?

Here's a person, I thought to myself, who has turned reality upside down, or at least the reality perceived by a large number of Prescottonians who look for, then see, people out to get them.

"How do you look at life?" I inquired.

"I see it funny. I view it as a series of candid camera episodes. I look around and see goofy people doing goofy things."

"How did you become so weird?"

"Well, I was lucky enough to have a heart attack eight years ago. I used to be one of those guys who took everything seriously, especially work. I put in long hours, was generally irritable, got aggravated easily and, for the most part, was the kind of a hostile, aggressive person who would step on anyone who got in my way. I was also miserable."

"Anyhow, after the attack, my doctor told me I would have to change my attitude and lifestyle or I'd be a prime candidate for another one. He recommended the book, Laugh after Laugh: The Healing Power of Humor by Dr. Raymond Moody Jr. I haven't been the same since."

"So what happened?" I asked.

"I literally laughed myself back to health."

"Explain that."

"If you've read several of Norman Cousins' books, you'd understand. Anyhow, I discovered that humor, especially when it includes laughter, has a marvelous healing power. The more I laughed, the better I felt. The problem was that all my friends were in the same old mold I used to be in. You know, serious and having no fun. When I was around them, my spirits were down, even when I tried to be cheery."

"So what did you do?"

"I decided to move to Prescott. There were already a lot of funny people here. And when I put on my special glasses, all the rest became funny too."

"You mean it's all in the way you look at things?"

"Absolutely. When I was sick, my doctor told me that the average American laughs fifteen or more times a day. It was extraordinary if I

81

laughed once a month. Now I'm way over fifteen a day."

"So, what makes you laugh in Prescott?"

"Hey, it's easy. Sunday I watch the tourists on the Square. Monday I sit in the YMCA lobby and listen to the folks who gather there. Tuesday I go to the city council session. Wednesday I attend Rotary, Thursday I sit on the Courthouse Square and talk to new friends, Friday I meet a regular group of loonies at Cuppers, and Saturday friends and I walk the trails around Prescott."

"And now you're healthy?"

"In the pink. I just train myself to look at the absurdities in life. I hadn't realized before that they are all around me."

"And you now believe that the world is out to do you good?"

"Absolutely. It's all a matter of perspective. What you have to do is expand your sense of humor, look for things that make you laugh and your world becomes friendly and benevolent."

"Any parting words for the rest of us?"

"Sure. Remember, he who laughs, lasts!"

Green beans cause stress

Mothers, if you have young children, you do not want them to read this column.

I have uncovered some incredible information.

It confirms what I have believed since I was knee-high to a nipper. Are you ready? Here it is.

People who eat green beans, die!

As a matter of fact, recent research, which has been suppressed by the green bean farmer cartel, indicates that 100 percent of those people who ate green beans prior to 1898 are now dead.

Furthermore, 100 percent of those who are now eating green beans will die.

There it is—incontrovertible evidence. You eat green beans, you die! Why?

We now know why? This information has also been repressed by the green beans cartel.

It is because green beans cause stress!

Not just your garden-variety, middle-of-the-road, give-you-a-cold-shiver stress. No! I'm talking high-risk, treacherous stress.

I began suspecting this a few weeks after my 4th birthday. I remember the moment well. As usual, I had refused to eat the green beans on my plate, nor could I dispose of them by slyly slipping them to my dog, Woof. She, being older and more experienced than I, had discovered several years earlier that green beans were stress-producing. She no longer even sniffed at them.

It was on this day that I decided to assert my rights. I pushed the plate to the center of the table (tumbling my milk glass in the process) and screamed my mother's favorite word, "NO!"

I then folded my arms resolutely and looked her square in the eyes.

For some reason, I can't recollect what happened next. The sequence is blurred because things moved so fast. But I do recall that ever since that day, green beans have been associated with stress.

But, listen up, the suppressed cartel study reveals several other fascinating bits of information.

No one has even been known to die eating chocolate ice cream.

Nor is there any record of a single person succumbing while partaking of German chocolate cake.

And, of the literally thousands of people who have ingested chocolate mousse, fully 78 percent are still alive, well, and exceedingly happy.

Further, there is no shred of evidence that any of the above have any relationship with stress—with one exception.

I was at a dinner party where chocolate cake was served. The lady on my left whispered to me (as she forked a huge dollop into her mouth), "Oh, I feel so guilty eating this!"

Being the gentleman that I am, I refrained from informing her that guilt is stressful. She was enjoying her dollops so much, I just didn't have the heart.

So, there you have it!

Eating green beans is stressful: eating chocolate ice cream, mousse and cake is not.

Unless you feel guilty doing so.

I have decided not to!

The concisers and the complicators

For lo these many years I have had some favorite words: Yes—No—Fine—Done—Okay—Lovely—Right—Super.

My favorite phrases run along these lines: You've got it—No problem—I'll do it—I understand—Consider it done—No sweat—That's it.

There are others in both categories, but you've got the idea by now.

I love short, concise responses. I lack the necessary patience for long-winded answers unless, of course, the question requires a detailed response.

What really tests me is the watch/clock syndrome. Ask what time it is and you become the victim of someone who explains how to build a clock.

Related to this are the people who have to make everything complicated. Ask them to color the banner black and that'll drive you crazy asking "How black?"

I can just about pinpoint when I began to have problems with these sorts of people. I was in the 5th grade. I asked the teacher how to work a math problem and, as a consequence, had to listen to a dissertation on the history of some obscure mathematical theory. My classmates and I went through the whole year determined never to ask her another question.

It wasn't a week later when I learned how much I disliked the excessive explainer's cousin the complicator.

It was one our Saturday morning football games on the neighborhood vacant lot. I was the quarterback so it was my responsibility to call the plays. As I recall, the meeting in the huddle went something like this:

"OK. Jimmy, you block Billy. Sam, you center the ball then block Corky. Bobby, you go long and Buddy, you go short." With five-man teams, that was the standard play. In fact, I don't think we ever used any others.

But I had failed to take into account Bobby Matthews.

"Do you want me to line up on the left or right before I go long? If I line up on the right, I might run into the two trees, but if I line up on the left, I could run over the hill into the street. So, which do you want me to do?"

"Left, and stay out of the street."

"Why? There's no cars on this street anyhow."

"Because the street's out of bounds, that's why. Now, let's go."

"OK. I'll go straight down for six yards, then cut right, then go long for ten yards then look over my shoulder. You can hit me with the ball then."

As I recall, I drilled him in the butt!

Years later, I had a second Bobby M. in one of my classes. I'd give a simple assignment then have to spend 5 minutes answering questions from a young lady. She also had difficulty answering questions. Oh, she would eventual answer them, it just took next to forever. I tried hard not to call on her.

The fact is, she wasn't responsible for my becoming impatient. She didn't have the power to upset me unless I gave it to her. Which I did.

It took me a number of years to learn this critical lesson. It has to do with control, doesn't it? I can give it away or keep it. I can give you the power to make me angry, or I can decide not to give you that power. It's my decision.

I thought about this recently when a friend went on and on explaining some theory that, to me, was exceedingly boring. I said to myself, "Boy, he is making me mad."

Then it occurred to me that I was giving him control of my emotions. So, I took the control back.

No one can get your goat without your permission.

It's a good thing to remember, I think.

I've improved in relating to the Bobby M's of the world.

Although, I know I'd do even better if. . . .

Encourage dreams

It's October.

Halloween is drawing nigh.

And I'm concerned about the health of whimsy, humor and human folly.

Specifically, I'm beginning to fear:

• That children are growing up without exposure to elves, goblins, gnomes and trolls.

• That fairytales are no longer the staple of family firesides, leaving youngsters unable to picture themselves cavorting in such yarns.

• That children's fantasies and imaginations and dreams aren't receiving enough encouragement.

• That family myths, sayings, tall stories are not being passed on from generation to generation.

• That the desire for goods are coloring our lives bland while we overlook the fun of trifles, trinkets and baubles.

• That human folly is undervalued and undermined when we turn away from what is humorous and frivolous and ridiculous.

• That we are becoming intolerant of impractical knowledge and unrealistic relevancy.

• That outrageous behavior has become the sole province of babies, politicians and ideologues.

• That humor is now being defined by paid professionals and that canned laugh tracks tell us when to laugh.

• That schools give too little attention to the encouragement of whimsy, and that human folly and humor are not celebrated and rewarded.

• That too many people are engaged in the waltz of somber indifference rather in the polka of life, and that we have forgotten Friedrich Nietzche's statement, "I would never believe in a God who couldn't dance."

• That people who fail to recognize that life is a glorious, mad adventure are missing out on the greatest of human follies.

• That the boat that leaves daily for the land of whim is rarely filled.

• That when folly is the alternative to calculated indifference, the latter will be the choice for the many.

• That the paths to wisdom are rarely walked by those who have not embraced folly, humor and whimsy.

• That solemnity about self, coupled with a grave disposition, is damaging people's chances to engage openly in whimsy.

• That the magic kingdom where whimsy reigns, folly is the court jester, and happiness is undiluted humor is being visited by too few young people.

• That Montaigne's words are not being heard: "The man too wise for folly is not so wise as he thinks."

• That the folly within this column will not be recognized as such.

Understanding language means looking for the melody

When I was a kid, one of my heroes was Tom Sawyer. There were days when I thought about becoming Huck Finn, but I wasn't cut out for the role. I was close to my parents, especially dependent-wise, and couldn't bring myself to ape his free-wheeling, non-conformist behavior.

Besides, we already had a neighborhood youngster who fit that role. He went where he wanted to when he wanted to. Some days he didn't show up for school; some days he would leave at recess and once he spent the day at the Kansas City Zoo — visiting friends, he told us. Whenever we saw a police car in the neighborhood, we could be pretty certain they were looking for Claude.

But as Max Shulman used to say, I digress! I have strayed from the real subject of this column which is Tom and Huck's creator: Samuel Clemens. I loved his books, but the older I get the more fascinated I become by the stories I read about his life.

And one of those I find most humorous centered on his communication with his wife and good friends. Put succinctly, his private communications frequently were filled with words that would be inappropriate for his books, columns and lectures. In other words, he was a big-time cusser!

It is also on the record that Mrs. Clemens found this predilection considerably less than appealing.

Apparently through the years she valiantly tried a variety of approaches to break her husband of his excessive and constant use of four-letter words. To no avail.

Finally, in despair, she lit on the inspired strategy of using the same words herself for a whole day — which she did.

Now as we all know, there are just not many things more galling than to try some dramatic strategy and get, in response, no response. But, as the story goes, that is what she got.

Finally, as they were preparing for bed following what she considered to be an especially inspired use of the vilest words she knew, and getting nary a nod of acknowledgement from her husband, she could stand it no longer.

"Sam," she said, "didn't you hear any of those horrible words I've been using all day? Don't they sound terrible to you when I say them?"

"My dear," he replied, "I heard them all, and I commend you on your splendid use of them. But I regret to tell you that even though you have the lyrics down well, you've completely missed the melody."

Unfortunately, history does not record Mrs. Clemens' response.

But Sam made his point. Unless you understand the feelings behind the words, they are empty.

Too many of us, I fear, get hung up on words when we should be concerned with what is behind them. Usually the melody is more critical.

Most of us struggle to express ourselves clearly. What we say is often not exactly what we mean, or we feel that what you think you heard is not what we meant to say.

Clemens had it right. Pay attention to the feelings behind the words.

We may not be good with the lyrics, but the melody lingers on.

Platitudes and banalities

"He is, you know, amazing!"

In one short sentence I have included the three most frequently used words in most everyone's vocabulary. I hope I never hear or see them again.

I am so fortunate to have grown up before the words, "you know" replaced commas and the thought process. And before "amazing" became a prime descriptor of individuals and things. Please, folks, can we all try to deep-six these shallow, inconsequential words? Can we agree that when everyone and everything is amazing, no-one and nothing is?

And while I'm in this reflective mood, I may as well share with you a few other pet peeves.

When is the last time you heard someone say, "Everything happens for the best?" Or that companion platitude, "Everything happens for a reason."

No matter how many times I have heard these little gems, I still flinch — which beats the cringing I used to do. Imagine saying this to someone who lost a family member in the recent Las Vegas shooting!

Anyhow, sparked by a short jolt of inspiration I began to jot down questionable maxims I've heard over my lifetime. Feel free to add to my small list. What I would really be interested in are those dippy platitudes I've missed.

"Every cloud has a silver lining." If so, I haven't found it.

"Experience is the best teacher." Frankly, I've met a number of individuals who haven't learned squat from their experience. They keep making the same mistakes over and over. Everybody has experience; it's what you do with it that counts.

"You can't tell a book by its cover." Well, I think you can if you read the dust-jacket. But, taking the maxim more seriously, I believe a person with only a moderate grasp of what makes people tick can tell a great deal about a person on first impression. Not everyone needs to examine the contents.

"You can't change human nature." Nonsense! I've seen people rise to the fullness of their potential and I've seen others move south to emulate their ancestors who still swing from trees. Education, perseverance and motivation are the critical factors.

"A bird in hand is worth two in the bush." This one won't be a winner with investment counselors. Many wise individuals prefer to forgo present pleasures or short-term gains for future advantages or profits.

"Eat, drink and be merry." This may make sense to an adolescent but

91

has little appeal to people who care about their health or hope to live to a ripe old age. I don't believe I've ever been acquainted with an elderly sensualist.

"Where there is smoke, there's fire." Here's a perennial favorite of gossips. It's also a dangerous assumption to make.

"Necessity is the mother of invention." Rarely! Most creative acts and inventions occur long before there is a need for them. Many inventors do their best work when they have the leisure to think, contemplate and explore alternatives without feeling the pressure of time constraints.

And finally, several that boggle my mind: "You can be anything you want to be." "Nice guys finish last." "Time heals all wounds." "Good things come to those who wait." Grrrr!

Are memories our most important possession?

What do each of us possess that may well be our most important possession?

How about our memories?

Because of mine, I consider myself to be one of the richest men alive.

Yet, I believe that many of us underestimate their importance and how much they influence our daily lives.

You might want to take a few minutes and reflect on this point.

Oscar Wilde once referred to memories as the diary each of us carries around with us.

For the past 50 years or so, I've developed the habit of almost daily writing a few memories down; ones I don't want to forget. I use picture albums to rediscover events and old friends. It is always astonishing what just one old photograph can call forth. A few of them have gone into stories or columns.

Of course, there are times when I don't want to make the journey back. I'm no more of a masochist than you are. My memory, like yours, is a personal history. We've all made mistakes, exercised poor judgment and made erratic behavioral choices. The best we likely have accomplished is to have learned from these decisions and put them behind us.

I am discovering—at my advanced age—that I am forgetting the names of individuals whom I have known for years. I was sharing this information with an old friend (I forget her name) several days ago and she exclaimed that this was happening to her too. We discussed the frustration we were both facing and the inevitable disappointment of drawing blanks.

But for the most part, my memory is an incredibly positive asset. I can't imagine how difficult decisions and judgments would be if we lived without the benefit of them. Our lives would be severely restricted and unsuccessful if we couldn't tap into memories.

Many of us old-timers have suffered personal losses. The loss of a spouse is part of my recent history and may be part of yours. I devote considerable time reflecting on her and our life together. The memories are easily retrieved and are vital to sustaining my mental health. She is—and will always be—an essential, beautiful and cherished part of my life.

For me, the older I become the more pleasure and affirmation I experience in traveling back into my past. When I'm "there" I inevitably spend considerable time looking around. I've always enjoyed sightseeing. I literally become engrossed in examining where I am and what I am seeing.

But regrettably, the trips are becoming shorter and the ability to maintain my attention span is diminishing.

And that reminds me of what a humorist once said about concentration: "I sometimes worry about my short attention span, but not for long."

Penny valentine heartbreak still stings

Remember those Valentine's Days when you were young?
How come they always occurred on a school day?
At least, that's how it seemed back in the 1930s when I was a kid.

I recall loading up with 5-for-a-penny valentines that I would give to classmates who were far down on my list of friends. Hallmark hadn't yet invented their line of classic smart-alecky cards or surely I would have selected from their clever stock. But to show my disdain, and in several cases, dislike, of certain boys and girls, I gave them my smallest, most insignificant cards I could find.

Back then teachers insisted that each classmate had to receive something from you. Everyone got rated and put in their place by the quality of the cards received. If you got some nickel cards, for instance, you knew you were very well-liked.

I carried two grocery bags on this particular day, one for dispensing and one for receiving. Such was my confidence that the latter was twice as large as the former. I anticipated hauling in the biggies. After all, I was class president of the Van Horn Elementary School fourth grade.

I arrived in the playground with my sacks, looking first for the obligatory kids who would receive my 5-for-a-penny cards. I wanted to get that over so I could really enjoy the rest of the day. We all did it the same way. We passed out our cheap cards before the first bell so we could enjoy the recesses and lunch period exchanging cards with the kids we liked. The better we liked them, the later in the day they got our cards. The best was always saved for right after school.

I knew the day wasn't going to be one of my best when the prettiest girl in class, Mary Ellen Benton, gave me a "pennier" before the first bell. So did 13 other kids. That was half the class. Had they forgotten I was their president?

But I was sustained by the expectation that half the kids were still holding their cards for me. That feeble bit of self-confidence got knocked over when all but Buster Wilcox gave me their cards at morning recess. He was my best friend; he held out until lunch. It was one of the worst Valentine's Day of my life!

The next Valentine's Day I still remember was when I was a high school freshman. In the 1940s, The Kansas City, Mo., school system had no eighth grade. From the seventh grade, you went right to high school. No transition, no time to gather yourself - you just got thrown in with all those big high school students.

I entered that forbidding place as the smallest boy in school, which I discovered on the first day when the huge physical education teacher ordered all of us freshmen boys to line up by height. I kept getting shoved down the line until I found myself at the end.

Maybe I should explain that I was, at that age, painfully shy and totally insecure around girls. Boys were okay, but Mary Ellen and some others had an impact on my fragile ego. I examined the ground a lot when girls were around.

Anyhow, during the fall semester I discovered a girl in one of my classes who was almost my size. I never got up the gumption to approach her or anything like that, but over Thanksgiving I began thinking that maybe she'd like to go to a movie or something. I decided to make my move on Valentine's Day. That's when I would win her heart. The high school teachers paid no attention to Valentine's Day, so I figured that whatever I did might be a big deal.

Throughout Christmas vacation, I considered how to ask her to be my Valentine. It was all I could think about, it seemed. I arrived at, and discarded, at least 50 potential plans. All of them had one big flaw.

I couldn't talk to her. I was just too scared!

But I knew Bobby Cox wasn't. He was then my best friend. So I went to Stover's candy store where they sold the best chocolates in town - they were the best because they were made right there in Kansas City - and bought a small box which I took to Bobby along with a "dimer" card. I asked him to give these two tokens of my love to Margaret.

Perhaps you can guess what happened.

Bobby ate most of the chocolates before handing them over to "my girl." Then before lunch they decided to go steady.

And that afternoon she handed me a "pennier."

Margaret and I hardly spoke during the remaining years of high school.

But that didn't much matter, because a few weeks later I spotted another girl who had a really friendly smile.

I was already planning to ask her to a movie.

Next Valentine's Day!

Reflections on a favorite author

I was rummaging through our home library recently and was somewhat surprised to discover that we had accumulated 17 early edition books written by Sinclair Lewis.

That discovery brought back memories of how much I enjoyed and appreciated the stories written by this Pulitzer Prize winning writer whose novels poked fun at the conflict of values he observed in our lives.

In thumbing through several of his books, I also was reminded of a trip our family made that was inspired by Mr. Lewis. If you recall reading any of his books I think you will appreciate this particular story.

We were living in Ames, Iowa, at the time. My Beloved and I had just finished reading "Main Street," one of his best known books, and after discussing it, we agreed that it would be fun to drive to his boyhood home in Sauk Center, Minnesota, which as some of you may recall, was savaged in this particular book.

Besides wanting to see for ourselves if the townsfolk had forgiven him, we wanted to also visit the museum that reportedly contained early Lewis memorabilia.

So, with our two small children, we set out on a cold, early October morning for the 300-plus mile trip to his hometown. Pulling into the small community we saw the first sign that indicated he had been forgiven — a street sign, of course, "Sinclair Lewis Avenue." We followed that street until we found downtown, which wasn't any great navigational feat as anyone knows who has ever visited Sauk Centre.

Anyhow, we found the museum, which was located in the public library. And then began a scenario that no one would have appreciated more than Sinclair Lewis.

We walked up to the counter and I spoke to the lady librarian: "Hello, we're from Ames, Iowa, and we're here to visit the museum."

"Well, it's nice to have you visit us. Now what is it you wanted to see?"

"The Sinclair Lewis museum."

"It's in the basement."

"Fine. May we see it?"

"I'm afraid I don't have the key."

"Can you get it, please."

"Well, you see, it's closed during the winter months."

The rest of the conversation was classic Lewis.

He would have loved it.

As for My Beloved and me, ever after, whenever we heard someone speak of Sinclair Lewis, or mention Sauk Centre, we smiled at each other and shared quietly a special droll memory.

The week Kuralt visited Prescott

Early fall of 1968 was a heady time for Prescott College and Prescott.

TIME and PARADE magazines did feature stories on Prescott College and a senior official of The Readers Digest was on campus. And to top that off, Charles Kuralt called to ask if he could "drive over" to film one of his "On the Road" segments for the Walter Cronkite CBS Evening News Program.

Those of you of a certain age will surely recall Kuralt and the "Road" series.

Our family had arrived on July 1 to take up residence in a lovely new home on campus. I had assumed an administrative position at the college. My first assignment was to be host to Kuralt and his assistants. Ron Nairn, the college president, had plenty on his plate.

Well, I have got to tell you, that week with Charley (he insisted we call him that) and his crew was a blast. They shot scenes — or whatever you call them — in the mornings, played golf in the afternoons, and we met for libations at our home in the late afternoons before adjourning for dinner. My Beloved and our two children enjoyed the time we had with them as much as I did.

And when the "show" was broadcast a few weeks later, we were all excited and happy with the program and the national exposure. There was also one unanticipated result. When Walter Cronkite's daughter, a recent high school graduate who had decided she wasn't interested in going to college, saw the segment, she told her father that if she ever did go to college, that is where she would want to go. Father Cronkite, who possessed rather strong feelings about her decision to skip college, acted with haste, calling Dr. Nairn, asking him if it was too late for his daughter to apply. The two of them flew out here the next day. She went through required interviews with a few staff and students, received blessings, and enrolled the following day.

If you're still with me, you deserve a reward. So here is one of my favorite "On the Road" segments.

Charley and his team pulled into a very small town in Nebraska and decided to stop over and talk to the local newspaper editor just to see if there was a story there. It happened that the editor, who had lived only in small communities, had a lifetime of musings about small towns. Following are some of them.

"You know you are in a small town when you don't use turn signals because everybody knows where you're going."

"You know you're in a small town if you're born on June 13 and your family receive gifts from the local merchants because you're the first baby of the year."

"You know you're in a small town if you speak to each dog you pass, by name, and he wags at you."

"You know you're in a small town if you dial a wrong number and talk for 15 minutes anyway."

"You know you're in a small town if you can't walk or exercise because every car that passes you offers you a ride."

"You know you're in a small town when the biggest business in town sells farm machinery."

"You know you're in a small town if you write a check on the wrong bank and it covers for you anyhow."

"You know you're in a small town if you missed church on Sunday and the preacher sends you a get-well card."

"You know you're in a small town if someone asks how you feel and spends the time to listen to what you have to say."

Dear readers, may your days ahead be full of love, peace, joy and a riotous sense of humor!

Let's not forget the childhood stories

I spent a few minutes last week driving slowly behind a school bus filled with our Prescott youngsters. Then two days later, I overheard two young boys talking about having to walk three blocks to catch the school bus. The experience provoked memories of when I was a kid.

Growing up in Kansas City, Mo. back in the 1930s and 40s was a tad different than what our young Prescott friends are experiencing.

First of all, there were no school buses to get us to and from school. We walked or rode our bicycles or, in really lousy weather, spent part of our weekly allowance (10 cents) riding the trolley.

But that was no big deal, because most of us had heard the harrowing stories of what our parents and grandparents went through getting to and from school. For instance my grandmother had to walk something like 75 miles to school and back. She had to fight bears, packs of wild dogs, eight-foot snowdrifts in May, and run the last 15 miles so she wouldn't be late to Miss Frankenstein's class. She feared her more than the bears and dogs.

My mother had it pretty good by comparison. She had to walk only 25 miles each way. She got by on one pair of shoes each year—cardboard inserts were a must!—and she received hand-me-down jackets and mittens from her older brothers. She and her classmates carried water into school from an outside well. Her clothes got scorched when dried on top of the wood-burning stove.

As for me, life was a snap. I walked only two miles to school and two miles back home. Both trips were up steep hills.

Today's kids might be interested to know that I used a pencil until it was too small to hold. My desk had an ink-well on it; I dipped my pen in it after writing every other word. Jeans didn't have zippers or designer labels and our T-shirts didn't have clever sayings or pictures on them and we wore laced leather shoes or boots except in gym.

Teachers ruled the classrooms. We were permitted to talk only when we raised our hand and received a nod from the teacher. Talking without permission earned us a half-hour detention after school.

If you're a kid reading this, I have several suggestions. First, go slow on being negative about your schooling. Your schools are much more welcoming, enjoyable, congenial, cheerful and friendly than most of the ones we attended years ago. I also suggest you ask your grandparents or great grandparents what their lives were like back when they were in school. But I wouldn't ask unless—or until—you see a twinkle in their eyes.

The best stories they will share with you only come forth when that twinkle is present!

101

The good old days

Travel back with me to "The good old days!"
I do hope you had some.

One of the memories I recall was the morally correct little admonitions my parents laid on me when I was a young whipper-snapper.

One that I inevitably received whenever I ran out of the house was "be careful." It conditioned me so well that I faithfully used it on my children. They may tell you that I still do.

One of my wife's old standbys, which she recited to our children every time they took a tumble or skinned a knee, was: "This is only going to hurt for a minute then you'll feel just fine!" She used to console our grandchildren with the same words.

But there was one I heard over and over when growing up that still arouses a strong negative reaction, if not a downright rebellious response. The provocative line is, "It's good for you!"

How many times did my mother use that phrase when I had on my plate dollops of green beans or broccoli or cauliflower or prunes or liver or some other weird-tasting stuff that young boys often dislike?

Now, I am well aware, as I believe I was back then, that she had my best interests at heart. Down in the deepest recesses of my slowly developing mind, I realized that those particular foods came under the heading of "health," but that didn't counter the rotten taste of each mouthful.

I think I was also somewhat aware that a significant part of my response patterns back then were directed at becoming less dependent on my parents. I was into challenging whatever they put before me.

If they specifically told me not to do something, the red flag of dissent began beating in my breast. It likely wasn't there before, but their words planted a strange spirit within that only the direct violation of their admonition could release.

Although I was unfamiliar with the poet when I was a kid, I now know that Carl Sandburg knew exactly what I was feeling: "Why did the children put beans in their ears when the one thing we told the children never to do was put beans in their ears?"

Like other youngsters my age, I was dedicated to testing limits. I was determined to see how far I could go in resisting rules and overcoming parental influence and power. I wanted to see what I could get away with.

To my mother's great credit, she usually helped me reason out my behavior. She would ask me questions that would undercut my childish logic and enable me to look at the pettiness of my arguments.

And never, no matter how infuriating my behavior, or how hurtful my words, did she resort to using that horrible phrase. "You'll be the death of me yet!"

Come to think about it, the phrase, "It's good for you," isn't so bad after all, is it?

Having nothing better to do

I want to say a few kind words about goofing off.

I first must acknowledge that I spent a significant part of my early years not feeling or expressing admiration of people who lounged around frittering away their time.

However, from my present perch in the retirement years I have learned to respect those who have embraced the art of malingering. I'm learning from them.

But I must acknowledge that I am not very good at it yet. I still lack the temperament to pull it off. I imagine there are a number of you out there who identify with me.

What many of us got good at was being useful, busy, efficient, punctual and resourceful in our effort to achieve success. Accomplishment was our goal. Sure our commitments gave us certain satisfactions, but they also stressed us out. We paid a price — and most of us know that now.

So today, instead of worrying about "getting things done," some of us who have reached a certain age are learning the noble art of leaving things undone. Many of the things that used to matter don't anymore. What are we going to replace these things with? What are we to do when upon awakening in the morning, we find there is no daily schedule?

Many of us grew up to become action-oriented people. We became doers. We got good at doing. But now, BEING is the new priority. Our character is getting called into question. And the rub is, character isn't manufactured overnight. We can't just wave a wand that changes who we are as if we were some old shirt.

However, we can learn. For the fateful fact is, real character is often associated with something old. Its development takes time. Those well-earned facial lines are significant imprints that distinguish us from those whose character is in the early stages.

What we need to learn is to appreciate being older. We need to understand that old homes, old cathedrals, old silver, old china, old furniture, old cars, old paintings are beautiful — as are old men and women.

But we won't see the beauty in ourselves — or anything else — if we can't slow ourselves down. We need to find virtue in being idle. We need to learn the art of ambling, of just sitting quietly, of lounging and sipping old wine. We've got to admire the snail and his slow, careful pace.

There's something about loafing that is glorious and magnificent. It has to do with time. And clocks — the absence thereof. It's understanding that the hours, now, are truly ours. We're in control, if we choose to be.

Instead of hustling to get somewhere and do something, we can sit back and ponder. We can work on our characters and not fret about becoming one.

Enough already. Nap time.

WISDOM

Betsy and Ron in Boulder, Colorado

Rational thought is not what drives us

"You're irrational!"

Anyone ever said that to you?

Did you feel like you had just committed a minor crime, or at least a major-league faux pas?

Well, you can relax. While there is a conscious rational mind that includes an IQ and deals with data, reason, analysis and linear systems, there is also part of our mind that is a creative place where our personalities, intuition, emotions and genetic predispositions come together to make decisions that determine what kind of life we lead.

What is important to understand is that you and I are primarily the product, not of the conscious mind but of the unconscious mind - the one that is below the level of awareness. It is our unconscious mind that really does the work of determining what we do and who we become. And this unconscious mind usually is not guided by rationality or logic. It is often irrational.

So we can be rational at times and irrational at other times, or an uneven mixture of the two.

Let me share with you a personal example that you might relate to. In late August of 1951, I returned to college in Virginia for my senior year. Walking across campus I saw a classmate and was immediately attracted to her. I arranged to meet her that evening at a convocation, then asked her for a date for the following night. By the third day, my roommate arrived and almost my first words to him were "I'm in love."

Now, Harry was a math major. He added stuff up and came to logical, linear conclusions. So he replied in a typical left-brain manner: "Are you nuts? You just met her. You've only known her for three days!" This was the first of many "interesting" conversations, but the reality is that he served as my best man several years later, and that the girl I glimpsed across campus and I have been together for almost 62 years. By the way, three years after our marriage, I served as best man to Harry, who married a young lady after a one-month courtship.

I think we all understand that loving someone is an irrational emotion. Committing yourself and your love to another person may be the most important decision we ever make. It is staggering to reflect on how little rational thought and objective analysis a goes into that decision. Yet it is a greater stretch of the imagination to think that someone would actually add up the pluses and minuses of a possible mate and then say out loud something like, "Well, it's 12 to 11, let's go ahead." If any of you out there

108

did pursue this risky method, I hope for your sake you kept your mouth shut. But then, I'm a romantic!

But it's not just love that provokes us to think and act irrationally. Old-timers might recall Vance Packard's 1957 "The Hidden Persuaders." This was the first popular book to expose the obscure world of motivation research, the psychological technique used by advertisers to probe consumer minds in order to control actions. Exploration of the unconscious factors that motivate people continues today, of course. The manipulation of our minds by advertising and merchandising organizations is an ongoing process. While we like to believe we are making rational decisions about what we purchase (appliances, cars, clothes), motivation analysts continue to tap into our minds to persuade us to buy the products they are selling. We may believe we are acting rationally when making purchases, but the evidence collected by motivation analysts indicates otherwise.

Our unconscious mind produces the thinking that shapes our judgments and gives direction to our lives. The unconscious is at the center of our behavior and primarily influences our passions, perceptions and the quality of our relationships with others. It is within the unconscious mind that a person makes most of the hard decisions that will affect the quality of his or her life. And we need to understand that this process takes place below the level of awareness.

Being human means we are capable of acting rationally and irrationally. Each of us has conscious and unconscious minds. And these two minds interact and influence each other. We are complex individuals and we should understand and celebrate this reality.

So the next time someone admonishes you for being irrational, just smile and say, "Well, duh."

That's an appropriate rational response!

True happiness is found in balance

"How are you?"

Probably no three words are communicated so frequently.

When addressed to those of us in our dotage, the "are" is emphasized, as in "How ARE you?" Most people are really interested, as in "Good to see you're still around."

No matter the inflection or degree of sincere interest, the intent is positive. To ask about our well-being is appreciated. And someone's caring is nice to hear.

Many of us respond by indicating that we are in an exercise program or on a diet or working with a financial planner. And we're sort of proud that we are taking charge of our lives.

But now, along comes a major study that challenges the assumption that most of us have made about our well-being. What the Gallup's comprehensive study of people in more than 150 countries reveals is rather shocking.

It tells us that what we have been doing to improve our lives may be either misguided or just plain wrong.

Or, in the words of Tom Rath and Jim Harper, authors of "Wellbeing: The Five Essential Elements," "Contrary to what many people believe, well-being isn't just about being happy. Nor is it about being wealthy or successful. And it's certainly not limited to physical health and wellness.

"In fact, focusing on any of these elements in isolation could drive us to feelings of frustration and even failure."

The authors go on to tell us that 66 percent of those people surveyed are doing well in at least one of the five elements that are essential to our well-being, but just 7 percent are thriving in all five. "If we're struggling in any one of these domains, as most of us are, it damages our well-being and wears on our daily life." In other words, we're not getting the most out of our lives unless we're living effectively in all five elements.

The study tells us that we may be better off not buying into programs that promise to make money, lose weight, or strengthen our relationships, because the evidence is strong that after spending the next few weeks dedicating our time and energy to a specific plan, we are likely to give up on these programs when they conflict with other aspects of our lives. The mistake we make, according to the authors, is in treating the critical areas of our lives as if they are independent and unrelated. They are not. They are interdependent. Again, the authors: "Well-being is about the combination of our love for what we do each day, the quality of our relationships, the

110

security of our finances, the vibrancy of our physical health, and the pride we take in what we have contributed to our communities. Most importantly, it's about how these five elements interact."

So, let's take a look at these elements that are identified as "the universal elements of well-being that differentiate a thriving life from one spent suffering. They describe aspects of our lives that we can do something about and that are important to people in every situation we studied."

The first element is career well-being. It's how we spend time during our working years and whether we like what we do each day. Only about 20 percent of people give a strong "yes" to liking their jobs. It's clear that those people who are actively engaged in their occupations have an entirely different experience than those who are disengaged. Stress levels are predictably higher for the disengaged who live for the weekends and dread the workday.

The second element is about having strong relationships and love in your life. According to a Harvard study, social well-being is dependent on our entire network of relationships. Having direct and frequent social contact with people who are happy and identified as having a high degree of wellbeing dramatically increases our chances of being happy.

The third element is about effectively managing our economic life - financial wellbeing. The authors verified what many of us know or suspect that the amount of money we have is not the best gauge of our financial wellbeing, let alone our life in general. While there are a number of issues in this section that merit attention, there is one conclusion that stands out - people who spent their money on a gift for someone else or who gave it to charity experienced a significant boost in wellbeing while people who spent the money on themselves did not.

The fourth element is about having good health and enough energy to get things done on a daily basis - physical wellbeing. Nothing too revelatory in this section of the book except an emphasis on the hundreds of moments each week when we make seemingly small, but eventually significant decisions that affect our bodies and minds.

The fifth element is about the sense of engagement we have with the area where we live--community wellbeing. It's about what we do to give back to our community. It's giving willingly of one of our most valuable assets - our time.

The challenge each of us faces is to maintain well-being in each of the five areas. The book takes a holistic view, as we should if we want to make our lives more worthwhile. I commend this book to you. And for those of you who are, like me, retired, take heart. We have only four challenges to focus on.

"Wellbeing: The Five Essential Elements" is available at the Peregrine Bookstore and the Prescott Public Library.

Share your story with next generation

"Read me a story," a child will insist.

And, as a parent or grandparent, we do. It's not just that we want to provide pleasure and learning, but we experience joy ourselves when sharing with a youngster words from a well-written book. Doing so is part of what makes our relationship fulfilling.

"Tell me a story."

Now, here is a more challenging and personal request. "From your lips," the child is saying, "share with me a story."

What a wonderful opportunity we are presented. Either we can make one up using our imagination or describe to the young person a story from our past.

And while tapping the resources dwelling in the creative part of our mind can be fun and entertaining, the more personal and meaningful source for potentially exciting stories resides within our own experiences.

For each of us has wonderful stories to tell.

We may not be born with the gift of storytelling, but we can learn. We can become exciting tellers of stories if we choose to.

It is as Jean-Paul Sartre wrote: "A man is always the teller of tales; he lives surrounded by his stories and the stories of others, he sees everything that happens to him through them - and he tries to live his own life as if he were telling a story."

Each family carries within it an elaborate collection of stories that spell out rituals, rites of passage and myths, which makes a particular family history unique.

One side of my family came to the U.S. from Germany. During World War II, my grandparents hid their heritage. They were fearful that discovery would jeopardize their safety. In fact, my great-grandmother, who had been born in Germany, did not step foot outside her home during the war. She feared for her life.

My best friend during those long war years was a Jewish boy. How fascinating and educational it was for me to be invited into his home and listen to discussion about what was happening in Germany to his relatives. His family stories seemed unbelievable at the time.

In later years, during the 1960s, I listened to stories of racial hatred and discrimination from the southern states. They, too, stretched my beliefs until I went to the South and experienced parts of the same scripts that I had heard earlier. There, I developed my own stories.

Within a family, a person's place is often defined by the script the family is writing. My friend John was destined to become a lawyer because his father wanted him to enter his practice. I remember Susan, whose mother decreed that she would marry a college boy, become a mother of at least three children and spend her life in volunteer activities. The mother wanted her own script repeated.

But my friend David was determined to write his own story. He rose above the miserable drug-centered script his parents were fashioning for the family and became a success in business.

Each of us must review the narrative account of our lives, toss out the trash and hold fast to the treasures that enrich us. It is in our personal stories that we find meaning for our lives. And it is in sharing our stories with others that we discover who we are.

Some of our stories sound false when exposed. Some are the result of faulty or selective memories. Others are damaged by exaggeration or creative imagination.

But within each of us are those stories which, when shared honestly with others, form the essence of who we are, where we come from and where we are going. Recovering these stories may require a detective-like approach. Just know that they are there, waiting to be found.

So when a youngster asks, "Would you read me a story?" answer with "How about if I tell you a story?"

You might begin, "Once upon a time, when I was just a little older than you..."

'Us vs. them' is crux of our problems

Back in the '30s, when I was a kid growing up in Kansas City, Mo., the radio was our connection to the world. We had a lot of favorite programs and one of them was "One Man's Family." The whole idea of being a family and what a family means has been major influence in my life. Still is.

But my concept has broadened. It now includes "The Family of Man." And it is increasingly clear that this family is in serious trouble. There are multiple forces, organizations and people, along with religions, devoting their time and energy to dividing our global family.

It is easy to feel overwhelmed and powerless against the huge challenges we humans face. Especially if we are led to believe there is no way we can create or recover a unified human family. Perhaps the most important question, then, is whether a united human family is possible. Can we men, women and children join together recognizing that we are all in the same boat facing the same human predicament?

Last week, we lost an important leader - a father figure to many of us. Nelson Mandela taught us powerful and critical lessons about forgiveness and reconciliation. He taught us lessons about accepting differences and emphasizing similarities as he urged us to understand the true commonalities of being human.

So, where do we begin to rediscover and recover the meaning of family and what it means to really care about one another despite our differences?

Perhaps one way is to share with you a little story I have carried around for the past 50 years. Its message is universal.

This is the story of a man who put up a sign, "Puppies for Sale." He no sooner had the sign up when a small boy appeared, wanting to know how much the puppies were going to cost.

The man told him that, since they were pretty good dogs, he did not expect to let any of them go for less than $25. With a look of disappointment on his face, the youngster asked if he could see them.

The man called "Lady" and whistled. Out of the kennel and down the runway came Lady, with five little balls of fur rolling along behind her. One lagged considerably.

The boy spotted the lagger and asked, "What is wrong with him?" The man said, "Well, the veterinarian examined him and he says there is no hip socket in his right hip. The dog will live, but he'll never be much of a dog."

"That is the one I want to buy," replied the youngster. "I will give you

115

all that I have right now, two dollars and eighty-seven cents, and pay you fifty cents a month until I get him paid for."

The man shook his head, "No, we will make a deal all right, but you don't want that dog. He will never be able to run, jump, and play with you. You want one of the other dogs."

The youngster very slowly pulled up his trouser leg. There was a brace running up both sides of his leg, a leather kneecap, and a badly twisted leg. The youngster said, "You know, I don't run so well myself, and he'll need someone who understands him."

This is where we must start if we are to deal with the critical worldwide issues that threaten our survival - with empathy. This means that we try to see other people in the world as "us." We cannot have empathy for people whom we see and treat as "them." If we are to become a truly unified family, "they" must become "us."

And what we must recognize is that this magnificent rolling ball of a planet is in serious trouble, just as our global family is facing enormous challenges. The worst problems imaginable, it seems, are now facing us - from the threat of nuclear war, climate disruption, poisoning of the environment, large-scale economic inequalities, loss of biodiversity, the threat of pandemics, proliferation of toxic chemicals, small and large wars, the constant danger of worldwide terrorism, increased widespread starvation and poverty, and more. So much more.

It is easy to feel overwhelmed and powerless against the huge challenges we humans face, especially if we believe there is no unified human family. Or that a unified human family is no longer possible.

I choose to believe there is hope for humankind. That together the Family of Man can overcome these threats and create a world that is both equitable and sustainable. I believe we can learn to accept differences as we emphasize similarities and discover how to better understand the commonality of being human. I believe in forgiveness, reconciliation and the healing power of empathy. And I believe in the power of family.

Sense of wonder adds magic to life

Once we discover it, we never want to lose it.

We hold on to it as long as we can.

But somewhere around the age of 12 or 13, most of our wonder is gone.

Oh, we still cling to precious parts, fighting off sarcastic challenges from friends and disparaging comments from adults, but by then many of the most cherished and personal elements have disappeared into the shadows of new realities.

Now, as adults, we look back and reflect on that marvelous young age when wonder was such an important part of our lives. We think about all those dazzling discoveries that only a child can truly appreciate - a red bird on a limb outside the window, the fiery beauty of a sunset, golden, wavy wheat fields that stretch for miles, the freshness of a morning breeze, the gentle lapping of water on the shore, the tall trees and low-hanging limbs that beckon. The joy of hearing and seeing something for the first time can never be fully recaptured.

Everything was new. Different. Challenging. Inviting. Great opportunities were waiting for us. All we had to do was grow up a little more, be prepared to say goodbye to moms and dads, then decide which adventure to pursue first.

But something happened. Maybe we didn't understand what growing up really meant. Maybe the wonder got trampled by real life. Maybe schooling educated the wonder out of us. Maybe the more we experienced and dealt with all those inexorably insistent forces that strike fear in the hearts of budding teenagers, the more we retreated from the world of wonder.

Most of us don't know what really happened. But we found ourselves spending more time coping with requirements and challenges outside of ourselves that demanded attention. We were introduced to logic and reason and consequences. Expectations were laid on us. We accepted them and were counseled that we must leave the magic world of wonder and prepare to enter the awesome, complex world of the adult.

From a multitude of sources, we were urged to grow up.

Some people, who had no doubt lost both a sense of wonder and their youth - and are likely envious of ours - told us to act our age.

We listened attentively, believing that adults know best. Now, we know better.

In our later years, many of us are recovering our sense of wonder.

Some of us are in the process of restoring the magic of life to ours. We are cultivating the gift of imagination that we put on hold years ago. We are reacquainting ourselves with whimsy, fantasy, and all those gnomes, elves, goblins and trolls that used to populate our world.

Most of all, the fortunate among us are recapturing and reconstituting our early childhood gift of curiosity. Without it, we know there can be no recovery of wonder. So we are trying to look anew at old beliefs, examine again cherished assumptions, study discarded philosophies and turn our attention toward the writings of forgotten sages.

In a word, we are reinventing ourselves. None of us can do this completely, but we can engage in the process with an enthusiasm and commitment that will cause us to explore new wonders and look at old ones in new creative ways.

And perhaps it is as grandmothers and grandfathers that we fully appreciate how important the recovery of wonder and curiosity are. For without them, we cannot empathetically relate to our young grandchildren except as dreary, aging adults. Without restoring the magic of childhood to our lives, we cannot appreciate and comprehend theirs.

Some precious seeds of wisdom only bloom and show their true beauty after being nurtured by years of care and love. And fortunately, some plants, like wonder, will sprout and flourish again after years of dormancy and neglect.

So, this Christmas season is a splendid time to restore life to the child within each of us and rekindle the wonder that is resting quietly within, waiting for the chance to energize, revitalize and grace our lives - and the lives of others.

To all of you - enjoy the holidays and have a great New Year.

Uncertainty is what keeps life interesting

Here we go again!

Beginning another year is daunting to many of us. An opportunity? Sure! And, inevitably, a challenge. Can we make it a better year than the last one? What can we do to make it successful? When it comes time next December to add up the joys and sorrows, what will we record? What will our life be like this year?

Well, life for some of us is a fascinating series of hiccups.

We plan, schedule, arrange, program, list, plot, calculate, collude, conspire, and design.

But no matter how much control we attempt to exercise, life continues as an ambiguous, capricious, often incomprehensible pattern of fitful, fractured happenings.

Life is often dominated by questions; it is short on answers. The best questions may be unanswerable anyhow. But they do elicit responses.

Life is often a series of unrelated moments. We move from this to that, back and forward, momentarily confused or glimpsing a small insight. Learning to live with disconnected uncertainties is a giant step toward achieving a reasonable degree of mental health.

Living a life based on perceived certainties leads inexorably to a dismaying denial of realities. Blind beliefs cause people to act uncritically. Certainties tend to lead to bias, prejudice, self-righteous fanaticism and dogmatism.

We are surrounded by people who bedevil and harass us with their causes and their grandiose schemes that will save us - so they say - from the hell of doubt. They are unsympathetic with our indefinite and poorly defined lives. They are uncharitable with our vagueness and fear of absolutes. They are rude toward our stubborn allegiance to questions.

To them, life is an unqualified, unconditional surrender to answers - a series of yes/no options. Life is not neutral or even complex. It is composed of clear rights and wrongs, obvious black-and-white decisions.

Ah, if living were that simple!

But it isn't. Nor, if truth be known, would most of us want it to be. It's the questions that challenge our spirit that keep us alive and on edge. It's tough questions that give us the chance of figuring out how to live. It's complex questions that enable us to live relevantly and boldly.

T.S Eliot said we live "by hints and guesses." That makes sense to many of us. The hints we receive and the guesses we make are often impractical, sometimes troublesome, frequently incomplete, usually

119

imperfect, but they generally provide us with the necessary, temporary road maps needed to fumble our way forward.

Each of us devises personal road maps. Hopefully, most of them serve us well. Living is an acknowledgement that most of what is anticipated on the road (year) ahead will be worthwhile.

Living is also a belief that more good will emerge from our "hints and guesses" than bad. It's a hope that our decisions will be more right than wrong.

Living is an affirmation that even though we may not exactly know where we're going, how we'll get wherever we're headed, or what we'll find when we arrive, the journey is worthwhile.

Living with uncertainty is okay. Living with questions is okay too. Deciding what questions are worth finding responses to is what's entertaining and enlivening.

Life is gathering information and ideas in bits and pieces.

It's starts and stops, "hints and guesses," happenings and hiccups.

That's good enough for me.

What a great year we have ahead of us!

MLK key to reversing racist attitudes

She was a student in a college class I was teaching in the summer of 1964. It was my policy to interview students individually in order to learn a little about them and to break down the common teacher-students barriers.

All kept their appointments except for Mrs. C.

In my class she sat on the back row. Although she took copious notes, by the fourth week she was the only one of 93 students who had made no contribution to the daily class discussions, nor had she kept her appointment with me.

It was a surprise then, to see her waiting to talk with me after class one day. After other students had left, she approached me.

"Dr. Barnes, my husband and I have talked it over, and we'd like to invite you and your family to our home this Sunday to have dinner with us."

I was a bit taken aback by this sudden invitation, but I told her I would discuss it with my wife and asked if she would speak with me after class the next day.

It was during the following class that I saw Mrs. C's eyes enlarge. For the remainder of the period she was in a state of great anxiety. When the bell rang, she made a beeline for me.

"Dr. Barnes," she began, "I didn't know! I didn't know!" Tears began to stream down her face. "I didn't know you were white. My husband and I can't ask you into our home. We'd be killed. Oh, I'm so embarrassed!"

I comforted her as best I could, told her how pleased I was that I had "passed" for a month, and that I surely understood why we should not be guests in their home.

You see, I was teaching at Tuskegee Institute, a black college in Alabama, founded by Booker T. Washington, and Mrs. C assumed any instructor would be black no matter how light his or her skin might be.

I was then chairman of the Commission on Higher Education of the Negro for the National Council of Churches. Since my assignment was to help plan the integration of traditionally black and predominately white colleges, I was teaching at Tuskegee Institute in order to learn firsthand about the problems the commission would face in the integration of colleges and universities.

Mrs. C. will forever be in my memory. So will the names of Chaney, Goodman and Schwerner, the three civil rights workers who were slain that summer in nearby Philadelphia, Mississippi.

Nor will I forget arriving in Tuskegee two days after the only black shopping center was burned to the ground while white peace officers prevented the black owners from hooking up their hoses to fight the fire. The local firefighters (also all white men) arrived "late."

Earlier that spring, the local high school was burned to the ground because it was to be integrated that fall. The Klan took credit for that action.

The Freedom Summer of 1964 was not a period of U.S. history to look back on with pride. But it is a summer our family will never forget.

Which is one reason why tomorrow is important to us. It is when we observe the birthday of Martin Luther King Jr.

In the struggle for civil rights in this nation, no person made more of a difference. His non-violent approach and his dream of freedom altered the course of American history. We do honor to ourselves by honoring him.

As I reflect on him and his work, I remember Mrs. C. I know we could now have dinner together in her home without risking her or our lives, thanks in large part to the work of Dr. King.

That's worth thinking about tomorrow... and every other day, for that matter.

Mental health is relative term for all

In the past several months it seems like I have read an inordinate number of articles about what's wrong with us. Some have illuminated emotional distress issues, others focus on our bad habits or how we are abusing ourselves. One can get pretty depressed reading this stuff, or even reach a conclusion that we humans might even be heading for extinction if we keep doing what we're doing.

It's all a bit much for me. Some people might be determinedly thick-headed and pursuing life on the wrong track, but most folks I know are doing pretty well. They aren't just surviving, they are making it! They are happy, confident, well-adjusted individuals.

But the articles did tickle a memory.

Back in the early '70s when I was on the staff of the Menninger Foundation, a psychiatric facility in Topeka, Kan., we worked with leaders of organizations - individuals who were doing well in their jobs and were well-regarded by their peers. Yet, they enrolled in our week-long seminar, "Toward Understanding Human Behavior," because they wanted to be better executives, fathers or mothers, husbands or wives - or just better human beings.

If you're reading this column, the chances are you are reasonably mentally healthy. Can you be better? Sure. But how do you know you are getting there?

Well, back in the early '60s, two psychologists at The Menninger Foundation wondered much the same thing. They became interested in defining mental health. So they asked 14 of their colleagues to describe five people whom they considered to be mentally/emotionally healthy men and women. Approximately 80 people were described. The two researchers then sought to find common qualities within these individuals. They discovered five common characteristics that, they concluded, identified mentally/emotionally healthy persons.

First, these folks were able to treat others as individuals. They didn't categorize other people. They were able to see the uniqueness of each person and were able to open themselves to the rich variety that different people offer.

Secondly, the individuals had a variety of sources of gratification. All of their psychological needs were not in one basket. They had a number of ways of enjoying themselves, of having fun, getting satisfaction.

Third, these people were flexible under stress. They could cope with problems in a number of different ways. When one method of solving a problem didn't work, they would try another tack. They could adapt strategies that enabled them to find alternative solutions to problems.

Fourth, the individuals were able to identify their strengths and accept their limitations. They did not depreciate their abilities and talents nor overvalue themselves.

And last, mentally healthy people were active and productive in a quality manner. They were active because they enjoyed what they were doing while their productive activities afforded them pleasure.

Before going any further I should indicate that being a mentally healthy person is never a static condition. A person is always in the process of becoming mentally healthy as opposed to being there. Or as Gertrude Stein once said about Oakland, "There's no there, there."

Becoming mentally healthy is a continuous, progressive commitment that makes life worth living despite all the miseries that exact their toll upon us. As a matter of fact is it probably through suffering and temporary defeats that we learn best to deal constructively and positively with the complex realities of our lives.

Need a little help in becoming a mentally healthy person? The late Dr. Karl Menninger, author and psychiatrist, gives us several guidelines that might be helpful:

"Set up as an ideal the facing of reality as honestly and cheerfully as possible."

"Cultivate social contacts and cultural developments."

"Recognize neurotic evasions as such and substitute hobbies for habits when needed."

"Learn to recognize the symptoms of your mental problems and how best to deal with them."

"Assume that the unhappy are always (or at least partly) wrong."

And finally, one more thought. We had a pretty good motto in the Center for Applied Behavioral Sciences at The Menninger Foundation: "You don't have to be sick to get better."

You just might want to think about that!

Chief Seattle's words speak of earth

This coming Tuesday is Earth Day.

In recognition of this important event, I hope you will read the reply of Chief Seattle to an inquiry by the U.S. government about buying tribal lands in 1852 for the arriving white people. The Chief's reply follows:

The President in Washington sends words that he wishes to buy our land. But how can he buy or sell the sky? The land? The idea is strange to us. If we do not own the freshness of the air and the sparkle of the water, how can you buy them?

Every part of the earth is sacred to my people. Every shining pine needle, every shining shore, every mist in the dark woods, every meadow, every humming insect. All are holy in the memory and experience of my people.

We know the sap that courses through the trees as we know the blood that courses through our veins. We are part of the earth and it is part of us. The perfumed flowers are our sisters. The bear, the deer, the great eagle, these are our brothers. The rocky crests, the juices in the meadow, the body heat of the pony, and man, all belong in the same family.

The shining water that moves in the streams and rivers is not just water, but the blood of our ancestors. If we sell our land, you must remember that it is sacred. Each ghostly reflection in the clear waters of the lakes tells of events and memories in the life of my people. The water's murmur is the voice of my father's father.

The rivers are our brothers. They quench our thirst. They carry our canoes and feed our children. So you must give to the rivers the kindness you would give any brother.

If we sell you our land, remember that the air is precious to us, that the air shares its spirit with all the life it supports. The wind that gave our grandfather his first breath also receives his last sigh. The wind also gives our children the spirit of life. So if we sell you our land, you must keep it apart and sacred, as a place where man can go to taste the wind that is sweetened by the meadow flowers.

Will you teach your children what we have taught our children? That the earth is our mother? What befalls the earth befalls all the sons of the earth?

This we know: the earth does not belong to man, man belongs to the earth. All things are connected like the blood that unites us all. Man did not weave the web of life, he is merely a strand in it. Whatever he does to the web, he does to himself.

One thing we know: our god is also your god. The earth is precious to him and to harm the earth is to heap contempt on its creator.

Your destiny is a mystery to us. What will happen when the buffalo are all slaughtered? The wild horses tamed? What will happen when the secret corners of the forest are heavy with the scent of many men and the view of the ripe hills is blotted by talking wires? Where will the thicket be? Gone! Where will the eagle be? Gone! And what is it to say goodbye to the swift pony and the hunt? The end of living and the beginning of survival.

When the last Red Man has vanished with his wilderness and his memory is only the shadow of a cloud moving across the prairie, will these shores and forests still be here? Will there be any of the spirit of my people left?

We love this earth as a newborn loves his mother's heartbeat. So, if we sell you our land, love it as we have loved it. Care for it as we have cared for it. Hold in your mind the memory of the land as it is when you receive it. Preserve the land for all children and love it, as God loves us all.

As we are part of the land, you too are part of the land. This earth is precious to us. One thing we know: there is only one God. No man, be he Red Man or White Man, can be apart. We are brothers after all.

126

Fond memories of Mom are invaluable

It's waking up sick and she's there holding my hand.

It's crying just after I skinned my knee and being held tight.

It's throwing my spinach into my milk and listening to her laughter.

It's getting dressed for the first day of school and not understanding her tears.

It's skipping kindergarten on a beautiful spring day, getting caught, and seeing her smile.

It's tracking mud through the living room and hearing her run the bathwater.

It's seeing her on her knees trying to find my pet snake which she never especially liked.

It's remembering how she looked when I got my first pair of long pants.

It's thinking about how interested she was to hear about my first day of high school.

It's recollecting how cool she tried to be when I came home from my first date.

It's reflecting how proud she looked when I got on the bus to leave for college.

It's wondering how she managed to tolerate my pseudo-sophisticated college ways.

It's being hugged and loving it when we celebrated my graduation.

It's never forgetting the look in her eyes when I said goodbye and left for Korea.

It's rejoicing together when we saw each other after I returned.

It's watching tears of joy as she welcomed a new daughter into the family on our wedding day.

It's marveling how young she looked when she held her granddaughter for the first time.

It's finding her sitting rapturously intent as she helped her grandson put together a new Christmas gift.

It's holding her tight and listening to her sobs when my father died.

It's sharing her last several years together as her health declined.

It's reminiscing on a life in which she gave so much to us, her family.

It's being a grateful son who remembers her with deep love on this Mother's Day.

From all sons and daughters to all caring mothers - THANK YOU.

A convenient scapegoat

Hopefully there are at least a few of you out there reading this who can still recall those Sunday evenings when we turned on the radio in our living rooms and listened to the comedy of Fibber McGee and Molly, Edgar Bergen and Charley McCarthy, and Jack Benny. At least I think they were on Sundays. My memory is often on a field trip.

But there are likely more of you reading this who can recall another comedian who caught our attention some years later. Flip Wilson. He hit his stride in the late 60s and early 70s.

If you do recall Flip's humor, it is likely because of his favorite line: "The Devil made me do it!"

A lot of young boys and girls back then owe a debt of gratitude to one of the funniest comedians they ever heard or watched. He provided them with a response when a parent gave them a hard time for some hijinks behavior. Of course, it didn't always save them from parental punishment, but it was worth a try!

Let's agree that it's not only the young who attempt to explain away negative or wayward behavior by laying blame on the "the animal or the devil in us." Many of us attempt to justify our actions by assigning such statements or behavior to our primate roots.

It may be temporarily consoling to blame the Devil for our animal nature or for our actions, but we still have the responsibility to deal with the humanity that is distinctly ours—the freedom to choose between good and evil.

Because we are free to choose, we are different from animals. They cannot be evil. This is purely a human characteristic.

And being human means that we must cope with the dark side of ourselves and struggle to offset our basest instincts with our humanity. It is our quest to live by ennobling ideas that contributes to making the world a better place for future generations.

Secrets to a longer and better life

An important book came out in 2008 that I just got around to reading. It's titled "Blue Zones." The subtitle is "Lessons for Living Longer From the People Who've Lived the Longest."

If you are at or near my age, the issues and recommendations probably come under the heading of "too late." However, most of us likely have younger family and friends who could benefit from this information.

I'll try to summarize briefly the most pertinent issues presented in the book. Some of the strategies to achieve a longer, healthier life won't surprise you. Others may.

The fact is the people who live in the Blue Zones do not live longer through pills, surgery and medications. Their secrets are found in the everyday things they do: the foods they eat, the company they keep, and their perspectives on life.

You are probably interested in where these four places are where higher percentages of the population are able to retain health and vitality well into their 80s, 90s and 100s. Sardinia, Italy; Okinawa, Japan; Loma Linda, California; and the Nicoya Peninsula in Costa Rica.

OK, here are the nine most important adjustments that author Dan Buettner, in conjunction with the National Institute on Aging and top researchers in the field, identify that may add years to people's lives. If you want more information on each strategy to live longer, read the book!

• Craft a personal mission statement. Why do you get up in the morning? What are you passionate about? What is truly important to you? Find someone to talk with who can honestly assess your life purpose and your successes.

• Simplify your life. Reduce the clutter and noise. Create a quiet space in your home where you can meditate each day. Slow down!

• If you belong to a religious community, take a more active role in the organization. Schedule an hour a week to attend religious services. Don't think about it; just go. The life-enhancing effect may be a function of how you attend rather than the fact that you just attend.

• Identify your inner circle. Who are the people you know who will support healthy habits, challenge you mentally, and upon whom you can rely in times of need? Schedule time with these people regularly. Build strong friendships with them.

• Make a list of the physical activities you enjoy. Don't exercise for the sake of exercise. Make your lifestyle active. Do what you enjoy. Walk. Make dates with people who like to be active. Combine walking with

129

socializing. Plant a garden. Enroll in a yoga class. Make your life a little tougher.

• Reduce the quantity of food you consume by at least 20 percent. Drop your dinner plates and glasses off at a charity and buy smaller plates and glasses. Make snacking a hassle. Buy smaller packages. Step on a scale daily. Eat more slowly. Eat purposefully.

• Limit intake of meat. Eat four to six vegetables daily. Showcase fruits and vegetables. Make beans the centerpiece of lunches and dinners. Eat nuts every day; they are the cornerstone of each of the Blue Zone diets.

• Buy a case of high-quality red wine. Treat yourself to a "Happy Hour" with a glass of wine, nuts as an appetizer, and a gathering of friends or time with your spouse. Take it easy: a serving or two of red wine is the most you need to drink to take advantage of its health benefits. Overdoing it negates any benefits you might enjoy, so drink in moderation.

• Get closer to those you care about. Spend quality time with family. Establish rituals Children love them. Make one family meal a ritual. Establish a tradition for a family vacation. Celebrate holidays. Put family first. Nurture family connections.

One final thought: A long, happy, healthy life is no accident.

Happy days to you all!

Living will: Live life well

Recently a friend of ours had a "Going Away" party. He had inoperable cancer. He and his wife decided to throw a party for his family and 250 or so of their friends. He wanted to say goodbye on his terms. It was a great gathering and a splendid idea.

My friend's decision to share his final thoughts with people whose lives he has touched provokes me to do something similar. My demise is not eminent and my health is okay. But I want to share some thoughts.

So, here is an addendum to the official "Last Will and Testament" which My Beloved and I prepared some years ago. This is my public bequest. It has no legitimacy legally. And it is not limited to our children and grandchildren but is intended for all children, everywhere.

I, Ronald E. Barnes, being of reasonably sound mind, hereby lease to children, for the duration of their stay on this magnificent rolling ball...

WONDER, which opens the door to learning.

LAUGHTER, which I beseech you to use continuously and with abandon.

ENERGY, which I hope will be in full supply for the rest of your lives.

COMPASSION, which I urge you to nurture and share wherever and whenever you feel it can help others.

LOVE, which I trust you will replenish then give away with no thought of your own need.

PRIDE, which I encourage you to develop in order to share with those who need more.

STRENGTH, so that you can carry on when adversity threatens.

IDEALISM, which enables you to withstand the inevitable realities that try to trample your beliefs.

SPONTANEITY, which gives you permission to be yourself even as you question your identity.

SUCCESS, in whatever you decide is your definition regardless of society's characterization.

JOY, for which you must find your own resources so that tomorrow you can extend it to others.

APPRECIATION, of diversity and similarities but mostly of the qualities of humanness that draw people together.

TOLERANCE, which enables you to love those you dislike while appreciating differences that make each of us unique.

INTEGRITY, which makes inner consistency the basis for healthy

131

living.

LEARNING, which you must continue if you are to combat creeping ignorance that threatens all lives.

TRUST, that you will treat this precious planet far better than my generation has.

And I encourage you to assault windmilled resignation and indifference with a quixotic lance so that the dragons of hate and prejudice as well as the monsters of hunger and poverty are diminished, if not banished from our kingdom.

Glimpse into someone else's reality

A close friend and I had a disagreement recently. No big deal, but it got me thinking about why we differed and why there is so much disagreement among folks of good will, not to mention those in public life who denounce and disparage those who differ with their political views at the drop of a sentence.

Anyhow, it seems to me that many of the arguments or disagreements we have with other folks is because reality, and our perception of it, may be quite different.

Let's take a look at this issue.

I think the first thing we need to understand is that our behavior is based not on reality, but on our perception of it.

There are some guidelines, even principles, about perception that might help us understand better why people disagree so often.

First of all, no two people see things the same way. I have my view of reality and you have yours. We can observe the same situation and provide distinctly different accounts of what we saw.

How you see yourself influences how you see the world. Your self-image colors what you see. If you're happy, the world looks pretty good; if sad or depressed, it appears gray.

Your view of another person affects your relationship with that individual. When you meet someone, you form an image of him or her that is uniquely yours. How the person sees him or herself or how others see him or her will likely be different from your perception. You will tend to relate to her according to your image of her.

How you see things is based on how you have seen things. Your own past experiences determine how you see present realities. Since you have experiences unlike anyone else, you perceive things no one else does.

You see things differently at different times. If you're a morning person, the world looks better and brighter than it does for the individual who typically begins the day slowly and numbly. Additionally, your perception of the world and life today is more complex than when you were younger.

You see what you want to see. If you believe men are essentially chauvinistic, each man you meet will likely fall into this category. If you believe people are basically good, you will tend to treat people similarly. What you see tends to reinforce what you want to see.

Your values influence how you see the world. From early childhood you have gathered together a set of values that guide your present views of

133

the people you meet and the circumstances of your life.

You have a tendency to simplify or complicate those things you don't understand. Your desire to understand things is so strong that when facing a tough issue, rather than acknowledge confusion you will either move to make the issue simple in order to grasp it - regardless of its complexity - or complicate it in order to convince yourself (and others) that no one can figure it out.

You learn new perceptions through new experiences. The catch is, of course, that you have to be open to new experiences or you don't learn new perceptions. We tend to reject new experiences that don't fit our preconceived views of reality. When a person rules out new experiences, perceptions solidify, prejudice develops and becomes reinforced as additional experiences and perceptions are rejected and denied.

Finally, you see things not as they are, but as you are.

Reality. It's all in the way you look at it, isn't it?

Kids' behavior reflects treatment

I spoke with some young parents recently. During the conversation, it became clear they were struggling with number of parenting issues. The challenges of raising two youngsters reminded me of what My Beloved and I went through decades ago. Times change, but the essentials of parenthood remain pretty much the same.

It's a wonderful and extraordinary adventure being a parent. It's also a tough, demanding responsibility. In the process of parenting, one learns at least as many important lessons as a child does. And one of the most critical lessons, I believe, is to understand that children learn what they live. Let's take some examples.

When a child lives with criticism, she learns self-defeating behaviors. She learns to look at herself and others negatively. She learns to condemn herself and others. Her world is seldom the one she dreams about. Her life becomes restricted.

When a child lives with hostility, he learns how to be resistant and how to fight. He becomes angry and has trouble containing his anger. He is likely to become an aggressive youngster whose behavior patterns get him in trouble with others, especially authorities.

When a child lives with ridicule, she learns to be shy and withdrawn. She is unlikely to see herself as successful or talented. Her sense of self-worth will be low. She will probably restrict herself to low-level goals rather than seek out challenging opportunities. Her future will be constrained and bounded by self-imposed barriers.

When a child lives with shame, he learns to feel guilty. Guilt is the most painful of all the feelings a child can cope with. Unfortunately, it is also difficult to recover from.

On the other hand, when a child is given encouragement, she learns self-confidence. The more encouragement, the more self-confidence. Every child needs all they can get.

When a child lives with praise, he learns to appreciate other people and the world in which he lives. He sees himself in a positive way and, in turn, sees others the same way. Praising a child is the best motivator there is to launching him toward successful experiences.

When a child lives with tolerance, she learns to be patient with herself and with others. The example set by her parents tends to remain with her for the rest of her life.

When a child lives with fairness, he learns a great deal about justice. His ability to cope positively with the inevitable injustices of life will be

135

enhanced and strengthened. His approaches will tend to be based on standards of fairness and justice.

When a child lives with security, she learns to have faith and hope. Secure as a child, she is likely to be secure as an adult.

When a child lives with approval, he learns to like himself. Parental approval becomes the first stepping stone to building a successful career and life. Treating himself as a person of worth and value enables him to treat others similarly.

When a child lives with acceptance and friendship, she learns to find love in the world.

Forming a positive, vibrant, personality is one of the greatest challenges each of us engages in. Parents are the earliest and most influential teachers in this pivotal process. It's an awesome responsibility, but worth every effort.

For a parent, there is no greater reward than to help a child grow into the kind of adult who will become a loving and caring parent.

Know-it-alls the worst of the worst

Almost 20 years ago, national syndicated columnist George Will wrote, "The greatest threat to civility - and ultimately to civilization - is an excess of certitude."

The statement bears repeating.

Our planet is increasingly menaced by religious zealots who believe the world and their role in it is clear and simple. They are convinced their belief system must be extended to the rest of the globe even if extreme measures, including violence, is required.

What we know about zealots is that they think and act in polarizing ways: good and evil, holy and profane, them and us. Our nation is still recovering from the worst attack on American soil ever perpetrated by monomaniacal terrorists who were driven by religious certainty.

One result of 9/11, and the subsequent threat of other organized religious movements, is a corresponding increase in our nation of conspiracy theorists and politicians whose rhetoric is inflammatory, unnecessarily divisive, and demonizes those who disagree with them.

In the words of columnist Anna Quindlen, "America has been hijacked by those who cannot tell the difference between opponents and enemies, between disagreement and heresy, between discussion and destruction."

Supreme Court Justice Oliver Wendell Holmes once expressed his contempt for the person "who knows that he knows."

The conundrum identified by Quindlen and Holmes requires us to recognize the difference between hard facts and soft facts.

Two plus two equals four. The sun rises in the east. These are hard facts.

It is the soft facts that cause the problems. We need to understand that when people enter the world of beliefs and opinions, reasonable folks can differ. As long as "soft facts" are acknowledged as such, they are unlikely to impinge on our beliefs and opinions.

A related struggle is to overcome constraints that a "little knowledge" places on us. We should be wary of people who behave on the basis of questionable assumptions: "I know" and "I am right," often accompanied by the implications, "I know and you don't," and "I am right and you are wrong."

Persons who polarize conversations with "right" soft facts are operating from a base of "a little knowledge." They have neglected to search as carefully for truth as they have for confirmation of their convictions. Cocksure individuals terminate exploration and examination too quickly.

Such individuals may be cozy and comfortable in their beliefs and opinions, but have likely closed themselves off from the mysteries and complexities that permeate our world while cramping their imaginations into small, tidy compartments. They risk becoming claustrophobic in a cosmos of ideas that is expanding exponentially and challenging belief systems daily.

Part of wisdom is becoming aware that no matter how much knowledge we have accumulated, we know very little, regardless of the subject.

We should also remind ourselves that the spirit of liberty is the spirit of not being too sure that we are right. We need to think about matters like these more deeply and ask ourselves, "Is that true?"

So, let's try get better at asking questions, more devoted to maintaining an open mind, and be slower to embrace absolutes and certainties.

And when we disagree, let us do so with grace and tolerance. There is enough venality and low-mindedness in the world without our adding to it.

Lessons learned during a long life

Through the years, we learn a great many lessons. Here are ten of the most significant ones I have acquired. Perhaps these will provoke you to pause and review those that have impacted your life.

• To love someone deeply, and be loved in return, is perhaps the greatest of personal blessings.

• Making choices and living with them is as critical to my quality of life as any other single factor. I have made some superior choices during the years and some I wish hadn't. I live with both kinds.

• I believe that intelligence is no guarantee of wisdom, nor does sensitivity mean I will be more compassionate toward others. Intent, purpose and commitment must be factored into these equations. I do believe compassion is more critical to my development as a human being than intelligence.

• One of the most valuable assets I possess is a sense of humor. Without it, I would not have won the heart of My Beloved, nor would I have weathered as well as I have the inevitable crises and downers that occurred during the past 84 years.

While I laugh less today than I did in earlier years, I am more sensitive to and appreciative of whimsy, irony, comedy and buffoonery which I observe in the human condition.

• Attitude may not be the most important quality in my life, but it is close. I know that I see the world not as it is, but as I am.

My perceptions of reality determines my perspectives on life. My attitude is the root of my perceptions, and thus, my perspectives. The challenge is to keep my attitude as positive as possible and not be defeated by the increasing challenges of aging.

• I must continue to work hard to find the good in the world, and I regret that I must continue to work hard to find the good in the world. Idealism is still my preferred attitudinal choice, but sustaining this complex perspective is an increasingly demanding challenge. I take heart in Dr. Hans Selye's statement: "Realistic people who pursue practical aims are rarely as realistic or practical, in the long run of life, as the dreamers who pursue their dreams."

• What I do not know is infinitely greater than the little I do know. This realization is not only the true source of humility, but the reason I embrace the goal of being a life-long learner. In this regard, I have been indeed fortunate to live with a person who has the same goal.

• The natural vulnerability of my childhood was followed by a

139

determined attempt to wear, during adolescence and early adulthood, a mask of invulnerability.

After these years of immaturity, I was fortunate to learn - with the help of My Beloved and friends - that vulnerability means having the inner strength to acknowledge weaknesses, limitations, uncertainty and confusion.

Understanding that I am a flawed, imperfect human being was a necessary step to seeking the forgiveness of others.

• Although a huge investment of time and commitment was necessary, I have been able to develop within myself a special place, which nourishes my spirit when the outer world seeks to disturb or torment me. My inner world is lively, comforting, supportive, astonishingly provocative, and is tuned frequently to the exploration of wonder and the nurture of curiosity. Even the re-runs in my internal picture show do not become boring.

• It is critical for me to believe in what Marian Wright Edelman calls the Fellowship of Human Beings.

The principle of inclusion - not exclusion - of people different from me is critical to my attempt to become fully human. Healing and love are more sensible, humane and necessary conditions for the survival of our earthly family than divisiveness and hate.

We are the sum of our choices

A Talmudic legend tells us that at a child's conception, Leila, the angel of the night, brings the fetus before God. The angel asks, "Will this child be tall or short?" and God decrees its height.

"Will this child be smart or not smart?" and God decrees its intellectual capacity.

Then the angel asks, "Will this child be good or bad?" and God is silent, because moral volition is not a matter of divine decree or a matter of predestination, but of individual choice.

Ah, choices! Here's another story.

The medieval philosopher Buridan had a donkey whom, like its master, was a philosopher. One day, rather than offering the donkey his morning bale of hay, Buridan offered the donkey two equal bales of hay. The donkey spent the entire day trying to decide which bale of hay to eat. But the animal could not decide which bale was the better one. This went on day after day until the donkey, unable to decide, starved to death.

To a large degree each of us is the sum of choices we make over a lifetime. Over the years, we've reached many points when it has been time to choose, to act. Sometimes the choice is right and appropriate, and other times we haven't made the best choice. But we've also learned that not making choices can lead to anxiety or feelings of helplessness.

We have also discovered that choosing carries a risk. So we decide to make a leap of faith or commitment which is likely better than starving to death agonizing over the options before us.

The French philosopher, Jean-Paul Sartre characterized life in our times as being "condemned to freedom." Choices constantly bombard us. At any given time we have a huge number of decisions and an escalating number of options to weigh and evaluate.

Fortunately we have help with moral and ethical choices. We don't have to make choices in this critical area in a void. Help comes from experience, convictions, relationships and moral values we have affirmed through the years.

Socrates told us that the unexamined life is not worth living. An old friend of mine, the Rev. William Sloane Coffin, writes, "It's not the unexamined life that is not worth living; it's the uncommitted life. There is no smaller package in the world than that of a person all wrapped up in himself." He makes it clear that for Christians, love is the core value of life. From Corinthians 13: "And now abide faith, hope, love, these three. And the greatest of these is love."

141

For those reading this column who are in the early or middle years of life, you would do well to internalize the message at the beginning of the fourteenth chapter of Corinthians: "Make love your aim."

And if you are an oldster like me, perhaps you can understand that the nearer the completion of your time on earth, one of the personal values that may be as important as any other is to end life with a soul more beautiful and full of love than when you began this journey. If your choices through the years have led you to this conclusion, you probably can look back and honestly say, "I have lived a good life."

Have a great new year, folks.

'To dream the impossible dream'

"To dream the impossible dream."

Recognize the line?

It's from Man of La Mancha, the beautiful and powerful musical based on the writings of Miguel Cervantes.

The marvelous writer also had Don Quixote speak these words: "The truth of a man lies in his dreams."

Dreams! What would a person be without them?

Where would the world be without dreams?

I believe most of us resonate with the words of Thomas Jefferson: "I like the dreams of the future better than the history of the past."

Each of us dreams-of an improved life, a successful marriage and career, security for our loved ones. To be dreamers of dreams gives us hope and enables us to amplify our faith.

It is through our dreams that we weave the tapestries that surround our souls and give meaning to what otherwise might be bland lives.

As we grow up and older, dreams often identify major themes in our lives as well as major developmental issues we are facing.

The very young often use dreams as a way of coping with the awesome world in which they are struggling to survive. Often a child is unable to separate waking realities from nocturnal dreams, or fantasies from daily thoughts.

To watch a child play is to see the fullest expression of a dream world become real.

For adolescents, dreams are a vehicle that enables them to break loose from the incessant challenge of identity issues. It is dreams that permit them to confront a mirror and see beyond the acne, braces and imperfect bodies.

A young adult dreams of success. "Watch me go, world! I shall be rich, famous and respected." Dreams motivate, even when daily hassles depress and disillusion.

Middle-aged adults dream about what might have been, until they realize that the real question is "What will I be? Will I be healthy, happy, loved in my later years? What have I achieved, and what is left for me?"

It is in the middle years that youthful dreams must be confronted and new ones devised.

Finally, in the later years, a person's dreams turn outward. Looking back, around, and forward, dreams focus on loved ones, children and community. A person may dream about leaving the world a little better place than it would have been without his or her presence.

It is perhaps in a person's later years that dreams attain a luster that earlier ones cannot achieve. It is then that more people have time for reflection, time to ponder the larger questions of life. Dreams can provide meanings as they make daily life brighter.

Henry David Thoreau wrote, "If one advances confidently in the direction of his dreams, and endeavors to live the life which he has imagined, he will meet with a success unexpected in common hours."

Dreams! Keep them alive.

So you can be!

The good life

So few of us have it, yet most of us aspire to it.

When it's within our grasp, it skitters away.

When we court it, it turns seductive.

When we seize one part of it, the other components often disappear.

In our early years, we don't recognize it is even an issue.

In our adolescent years, with too many problems to distract us, it seldom enters our consciousness.

As young adults, we get occasional glimpses of it, but building a career and starting a family are higher priorities.

In the middle years, it gets periodic lip service but infrequent attention. We begin to understand it is important but we have not yet formed a clear internal diagram on how to make it meaningful in our lives.

For most of us, by the time we recognize how significant it is, we have forfeited our ability to comprehend its value.

The dilemma is that only if we begin early in life-when we are forming the guidelines by which we will live-can we bring it into sufficient focus to integrate it into our lives.

I am writing about balance.

It's the harmony of our intelligence, our physical selves, our emotional being, and our spiritual consciousness that becomes our whole entity called "Me."

When we neglect developing any part of ourselves, we pay for it one way or another.

We risk losing the ability to appreciate whatever part of the world we are avoiding or denying.

If we fail to develop our intelligence, we will decline in our ability to comprehend the changing world in which we live.

If we neglect the physical part of ourselves, our bodies send urgent messages until they are overwhelmed by abuse.

If we disregard the emotional side, we lose the ability to see the rich colors and hear the magnificent music that enriches our world.

If we ignore the spiritual side, we confine ourselves to self-imposed walls that hide the soul from the real treasures of the world that lie just beyond our temporal understanding.

It is possible that true wisdom only comes to those who have achieved a reasonable blending of these four elements.

It is also possible that a major part of wisdom is recognizing that a perfect combination is impossible, and that the best we can do is to work at putting these four critical components of self into balance.

Part of wisdom may also reside in convincing the younger generation who are struggling with the daily forceful exigencies of studying or making a living that they will only be able to achieve a balance if they begin nurturing it early.

Perhaps few other priorities of a parent or older friend or grandparent can make as much difference as effectively conveying to a young person that working toward balance is a key goal in life.

And that living the "Good Life" later is predicated on preparing for it now.

Memories

Here I am in my mid-80s staring at our computer reflecting on two authors whose books I read back in the '60s.

Old-timers may recall these two individuals - Harry Golden and Eric Hoffer. The two books I want to read again are Golden's "Only in America" and Hoffer's "The True Believer." I wish I had kept copies of Golden's newspapers in which he wrote each month, "The Carolina Israelite." I loved reading his stories.

But I guess the real issue of this narrative is to reaffirm for myself how important memories are to me. Perhaps they are the most important possession I own. Have any of you readers thought of them that way?

I believe it was Oscar Wilde who referred to memories as the diary each of us carries around with us. That's how I look at them anyway, even though a diary implies that I am writing them down.

And in a way I am. I make notes for columns and every day I spend time thinking back over certain times in my life or remembering people like Golden and Hoffer, and places that My Beloved and I visited. I don't want to lose my capacity of bringing those memories back to life. Sometimes I recover events and incidents that I thought were lost to me, and I can actually "see" what happened back then.

Then there are those precious days - like our anniversaries - when Betsy brings forth our picture albums and together we share the memories and reflect on those days and years past. Other times a movie scene or a line in a book will trigger a specific memory that we shared.

Of course, not all memories are pleasant. There are too many moments and times that are best left covered and hidden. So I am selective. I am not a masochist. I know my personal history is filled with mistakes and poor choices. I hope I have learned from them, but a visitation is unappealing.

What I have learned is that memories are an incredible tool. I know how difficult decisions and judgments would be if I tried to live without the benefit of them. Experience would be pretty ineffective if I failed to mine this resource.

So, I try to give them an appropriate priority. At my age this has become a challenge since my power of concentration is not what it used to be.

But I am fortunate. I can still find humor when I seem to most need it. Like recalling what a humorist (I forget which one!) wrote about concentration: "I sometimes worry about my short attention span, but not for long."

A Teacher's Creed

I was rummaging through some old boxes recently and stumbled across something I wrote back in the early sixties when I was teaching at a university.

I called it "A Teacher's Creed." It was my attempt to put into writing what I believed in and what I wanted to somehow share with my students.

I believe in tomorrow.

Today is my work bench from which I shall prepare students to live fully and capably in the world they will inhabit.

I believe in fun and play.

I shall try to make learning as joyous and exciting as possible for my students deserve no less.

I believe that ignorance is an intolerable condition.

With all my resources, I shall strive to combat it in order to elevate intelligence and insure that reason will prevail. However, I am aware that pure rationality without sensitivity may produce a form of ignorance unacceptable to a civilized society.

I believe in a learning partnership.

I, as a more experienced learner, commit myself to assist younger learners to discover what is good and useful. I shall try to stimulate students to join with me in exploring the unknown in order to discover more than either of us could have done independently.

I believe in the dignity of each student.

I shall uphold each student's right to grow and develop as an individual, and assist them to set learning goals, find resources, and evaluate experiences.

I believe in the excitement of learning.

I shall try to build on each student's curiosity and wonder as I communicate my enthusiasm toward learning opportunities. No pupil will leave my classroom less excited than when he or she entered.

I believe that knowledge is not enough.

The sum of what is now known does not equal wisdom. I must assist students to understand what they learn so they can use this knowledge to benefit themselves and others.

I believe that human values are of the highest priority.

I shall assist students to examine values, which enhance life and civilize humankind while encouraging them to continue building and revising their own value systems.

I believe that learning and living are synonymous terms.

Students will be encouraged to become active learners throughout their lives, thus I must help them understand that learning to learn is as high a priority as any other educational goal.

I believe that each student must develop a sense of potency in dealing with the world.

I shall try to help each student to behave in a manner that reflects a sense of power and creativity over what happens in his or her present or future interactions in their world.

I believe that each student must develop an awareness of self.

I shall assist students in discovering their talents and abilities, developing a heightened awareness of their emotional, sensory and bodily states, and feel positive about their potential as a growing, developing person.

I believe in the value of experience.

I shall assist students to understand that all learning results from and is part of their emotional, spiritual, intellectual and physical experiences.

I believe in the power of humor.

I shall attempt to maintain my own perspective by the liberal use of humor and share it with students when appropriate. I shall try to make laughter a major learning force in my classroom.

I believe in hope, love and kindness.

I shall extend these three elements to my students continuously.

I believe that patience is a virtue.

I shall nurture, cultivate and use it daily, sharing it with my students even when it is in short supply.

Perfection, don't take it too seriously

There is nothing wrong with perfection, as long as no one takes it too seriously.

Especially when the subject is people.

One of the most featherbrained phrases I hear uttered from time to time comes from coaches: "I want my boys to give 110 percent!"

How stupid and silly!

That kind of expectation is doomed to failure. No human, regardless of expertise in any area, can achieve 100 percent, much less 110 percent.

Whatever happened to the idea of doing your best?

That leads me to the role of parenting and the inherent imperfection.

There are no perfect parents. Never have been, never will be.

Even if a mother or father puts forth maximum effort to be responsive, loving, caring and conscientious, she or he won't come close to perfection.

But each of us can strive to do our best.

There are plenty of sources to help us, such as books and articles, parents, friends, courses and seminars. We can learn a lot about being a good parent, but what it boils down to is making the effort.

And one special key to that is try to understand the child within ourselves.

Childhood feelings are never outgrown; they are just hidden behind our adult facade.

Each of us has within ourselves the child we were at different ages. I can be in touch with "me" when I was 5, 8, 12 or 15.

A primary challenge for parents is to get in touch with the child they once were in order to understand and communicate with their youngsters. It's really the only effective way of putting themselves into the world of their youngsters in order to see the world through their eyes.

Unfortunately, some parents lose touch with the child that is within themselves. They have either repressed their childhood and early memories or are so committed to maintaining a stern unemotional adult role that they cannot relate to or identify with their children.

That's too bad! Those parents who have forgotten what it was like being a child will find it difficult to become closely involved with their children. Their "adult" perspective closes out their "child" perspective.

Perhaps in their eyes, being a good adult takes precedence over being a good parent. Of course, the ideal goal is to be both.

So, to become a better parent-not perfect, mind you-it is important to "go back" to the age of your children in order to appreciate what they are going through. Old scrapbooks and photo albums are one good source.

But keep in mind that while you are always a parent to your children, they are not always a child to you. To be treated as an adult by parents is a goal of every child.

Be aware, too, that as your child reaches adulthood, and especially after they become parents, they will begin to accept the reality that you were not a perfect parent, and never will be.

Hopefully, they will also realize that as a parent you did the best you could do.

The will

There are a great many folks in the Prescott area thinking about the following topic.

So this one is for you: a document I have kept for the last 50 years.

Every so often I pull it out to reread. You may find yourself doing the same thing.

A lawyer's last will:

I, Charles Lounsberry, being of sound and disposing mind and memory, do hereby make and publish this, my last will and testament, in order, as justly may be, to distribute my interest in the world among those succeeding me:

That part of my interest which is known in law and recognized in the sheep-bound volumes as my property, being inconsiderable and of no account, I make no distribution of this in my will. My right to live, being but a life estate, is not at my disposal, but these things accepted, all else in the world I now proceed to device and bequeath.

ITEM: I give to good fathers and mothers, in trust for their children, all good little words of praise and encouragement and all quaint pet names and endearments and I charge said parents to use them justly, but generously, as the needs of their children shall require.

ITEM: I leave to children inclusively but only for the term of their childhood, all and every flower of the field and blossoms of the woods, with the right to play among them freely, according to the customs of children, warning them at the same time about thistles and thorns. And I devise to children the banks of the brooks and the golden sands beneath the waters therein, and the white clouds that float high over the giant trees.

And I leave to children the long, long days to be merry in a thousand ways, and the night and the train of the Milky Way to wonder at, but subject, nevertheless, to the rights hereinafter given to lovers.

ITEM: I devise to boys, jointly, all the useful idle fields, all pleasant waters where one may swim, all snow clad hills where one may coast, all streams and ponds where one may fish, or where, when grim Winter comes, one may skate, to hold the same for the period of their boyhood, and all meadows with clover blossoms and butterflies, thereof; the woods with their appurtenances, the squirrels and birds, the echoes and strange noises and all distant places which may be visitant, together with the advantages there found. And I give to said boys, each his own place at the fireside at night, with all the pictures that may be seen in the burning wood, to enjoy without let or hindrance, and without encumbrance or care.

ITEM: To lovers I devise their imaginary world, with whatever they may need, as the stars of the sky, the red roses by the wall, the bloom of the hawthorn, the sweet strains of music and aught else that they may desire to figure to each other the lastingness and beauty of their love.

ITEM: To young men, jointly, I devise and bequeath all boisterous and inspiring sports of rivalry, and I give them the disdain of weakness and undaunted confidence in their own strength. Though they are rude, I leave them the power to make lasting friendships, and of possessing companions, and to them, exclusively, I give all merry songs and grave choruses to sing with lusty voices.

ITEM: To those who are no longer children or youths or lovers, I leave memory, and other poets, if there may be others, to the end that they may live the old days over again, freely and fully, without tithe or diminution.

ITEM: To our loved ones with snowy crowns, I bequeath the happiness of old age, the love and gratitude of their children, until they fall asleep.

Note: This strange will was left by a young lawyer who died some years ago in a ward for the insane in the almshouse of Cook County, Illinois. The will was found in his coat. On a resolution of the Chicago Bar Association, the document was sent to probate and was spread on the records of Cook County.

Workaholics

I suspect most of us in our lifetimes have known a work addict or two. Some of you reading this may fit that descriptor.

During my life, I consulted with many of them and their spouses, worked with their organizations, conducted seminars for them-all in an attempt to help them bring more balance into their lives.

Some made the necessary changes, most didn't. The latter were addicted.

Unfortunately, mainstream society not only endorses their addiction, but encourages and rewards it.

Every year across this country in many cities, members of the business community choose their "Business Person of the Year." Much too often, it is someone who works 80-90 hour week and expects his or her staff to do the same.

Everyone applauds and says the individual is a success.

Everyone, that is, except that person's spouse and children. They look upon him or her as an absentee spouse and parent. Or as one youngster said to me about his father, "He boards here occasionally."

Years ago when I was with The Menninger Foundation, we held five-day seminars for these "successful" executives. Many came full of themselves, proud of their successes, thinking they would confirm their behavior by comparing themselves-favorably, of course-with their fellow participants.

They didn't get what they expected. During the week, their attitudes were challenged, their concept of "success" was questioned, their priorities were scrutinized and their lives underwent considerable examination.

They accomplished most of this themselves; the staff facilitated the process. Removed from their comfortable, reinforcing network of business associates-their standard source of approval-they were unable to slide away from difficult questions about the patterns of their lives.

They had to think about themselves differently and look at their spouses and children in a new light. It became necessary to face the consequences of their work addictions, often for the first time.

Most took tentative, turn-around steps by discussing priorities and looking at how their life-styles were affecting others, especially their families.

They began to examine the reasons behind their addictive behavior.

Primarily, they had to explore their values and what was really important in their lives. Up to then, the answer was work. Spouse, children, self all got secondary positions. Workaholism was their bag; their organization was indispensable to them. They were compulsive.

One executive put it this way: "Somehow I thought I could catch up. I mean, my children were grown, yet I thought I could go back and recover those years I missed."

Addiction is like that. It blots out a lot. It produces strange reasoning patterns,

But it can be licked if workaholics really want to change.

Of course, they'll need a little help from their friends.

Keep on 'playing' in life

Travel back to me to those glorious days when the world was our playground.

When we played!

It was what we did best as children.

No one had to teach us how to do it. Indeed, when adults tried they were often ignored.

It just came naturally to us because it was such fun.

Then we went to school. The right-brained world of play began to get overwhelmed by the left-brained world of school. What came spontaneously and gave us pleasure began to be replaced by lessons and assignments, which adults said were "good or us." Mostly we accepted (as we had to) these admonitions, but secretly believed we were being conned.

But gradually we became conditioned. The amount of time we spent playing decreased; the time we spent working-for that is how we regarded school-increased. The new realities of what the adult world was about began to sink in. Play was what carefree youngsters did; work is what responsible adults did.

It was a lousy lesson to learn!

After learning to do something well (play) and just about the time we got good at it, we were told that work, not play, was what we better got good at. We were told that we must become adept at accomplishing something. What came so easily to us, gave us enjoyment and a sense of worth, and early on provided self-esteem, even a sense of identity, was now regarded as frivolous and non-productive behavior.

"You don't have time for play anymore. You must get serious about life," was the message communicated from all directions.

No wonder so many adults live lives that are no fun!

Lose the capacity to play and your world loses color.

Repress your humor and your emotions likely wither.

Stifle your particular brand of creative play and your perspective becomes warped.

Ignore the foolishness that surrounds you and your ability to laugh becomes impaired.

Regard work as the raison d'être of your existence and the non-goal directed behavior that is play becomes subverted by the pressurized goals of achievement until play and work become totally separate, polarized pursuits.

157

Yet, despite all this conditioning there are those resisters who manage to combine work and play in their businesses and others who successfully balance them in their lives. They have learned how to work smart and play well. Their capacity for wonder, innate curiosity, along with an unabashed love of fun remain alive because these childlike qualities are nourished daily.

These are the kind of folks who have decided that life is indeed too short to be dedicated primarily or solely to serious, sober, stultifying endeavors.

For them, play is a high priority; it is a mandatory inclusion in all aspects of their lives, not an elective. It is required for balance. For them, the fun that play provides is as important as their achievements within their careers.

They have discovered that the benefits of play contribute to their health, as a number of physicians and psychologists have been telling us for years.

Just as kids need play, so do adults.

So, as we begin a new year, let's put a little more fun into our lives.

Play will do that-if we take it seriously!

Happiness

"Happiness is winning the lottery."
"Happiness is having all the money I want."
"Happiness is becoming famous."
"Happiness is living a life of comfort."

The pursuit of happiness has always been a subject of interest to humans. Great thinkers, from Plato to Peanuts creator Charles Schultz, have cogitated about it and written reams of material trying to explain it.

Imagine how those thinkers would react to the above definitions!

I suspect most would conclude that civilization has stagnated. Suspecting such juvenile interpretations of happiness to be shared by the majority of the population, philosophers would only despair at the direction society has taken.

Even worse than accepting as a norm the contemporary concept of happiness as comfort, pleasure and material things is the passing along of this vegetative behavior to our children and grandchildren. It's as if we are saying to the young, "Seek wealth, ease, diversion and the goal of having all your wishes satisfied and all your hopes fulfilled."

The "Good Life," as generally defined, is one of total gratification, be it instant or long range.

But as the great thinkers have long understood, equating happiness with gratification is bankrupt. It always has been. With an unprecedented number of our citizens indulging themselves in unrestrained pleasure and comfort, still the problems of drugs, addictions, suicides and crime among these same people are endemic.

If they are achieving wealth, accompanied by unlimited leisure and self-indulgence, why aren't they happy?

The fateful fact is happiness has little to do with servicing one's desires and fulfilling selfish gratifications.

Years ago when I was on the staff of a university my wife and I invited a group of students into our home every other week during the school year to discuss issues of their choosing that were not being tackled in their classes. The very first topic they put on the agenda was "Happiness: What is it?"

After several hours of intense conversation they concluded that happiness was not something to be pursued, but a by-product of how one lives his or her life.

I am still—after many years—in agreement with them.

It is not a state you arrive at, but a manner of traveling.

159

Happiness occurs when a person strives to achieve meaningful goals. It doesn't mean attaining them necessarily. One can work to eliminate prejudice, upgrade local government, reduce the impact of drugs or decrease the incidence of child abuse, and be sustained by small victories without winning the war.

Happiness results when a person realizes that his or her commitments go beyond self-serving goals. Volunteering as a Big Brother or Big Sister, helping with church programs, becoming a better parent, assisting with voter registration, raising money to feed hungry children—whatever relates one to a larger context of purposes than those bounded by self.

Happiness flows from giving love, as well as receiving it.

Happiness comes from understanding that though we are selfish and egocentric, each of us is capable of sustained selflessness.

Happiness is an outgrowth of helping young people comprehend that the artificialities of life, as portrayed by much of the media, do not lead to a rich and satisfying life. As the young free themselves from the bonds of self-indulgence, they may begin to visualize a world in which they can make meaningful contributions.

They will see that world if it is part of their vision.

And perhaps the young will grasp the wisdom of Carl Sandburg: "I am an idealist. I don't know where I am going but I am on my way."

Or, William Saroyan: "The greatest happiness you can have is knowing that you do not necessarily require happiness."

And we extend to all children Adam Smith's benediction: "May your happiest days of the past be your saddest days of the future."

Differences

Sometimes I wonder if the differences between us can ever be resolved. We have so much in common, but it's the differences that get our attention and seem to identify who we are. The media thrives on pointing out our dissimilarities, contrasting beliefs and contrariness, behavioral discrepancies and incompatibilities.

Well, I suggest we devote at least some of our attention today to thinking about what we have in common. So I shall spend a few moments discussing the one thing we are all doing, cosmetic ads to the contrary.

I acknowledge that not too many of you will be interested in the topic unless you are wine tasters, antique dealers or trust officers of banks.

In fact, I'm convinced society believes it's in poor taste despite the reality that 10 out of 10 of us are still doing it.

Know what I'm referring to?

Aging, that's what! While few of us get too excited about it, we are all moving inexorably forward, slowly but surely. Frankly, I find the process intriguing, so let's begin by looking at three of the major identity statements which best describe us during three stages of our lives.

For adolescents, whose primary problem or stress is the search for identity, the best descriptor is "I am!" Further, "I am what I can make work," for so few things seem to work for the teenager. Their struggle for an identity explains their concern about clothes and their preoccupation with their iPads, iPods or whatever those little thingies are called this month. The salient point is they help them define themselves.

A major part of establishing their identity and answering the question, "Who am I?" is to make the move from dependency (on parents) to independence. While difficult for most adolescents, as well as parents, this transfer of primary allegiance from parents to peers must be accomplished if the teenager is to move on to the next phase of life, becoming a young adult.

It is during the young adult stage, (age approx. 20-39) that the next major identity statement is articulated: "I will be." "I will be successful, I will be President, I will have that home on the lake in the mountains, I will do this, do that—watch me go, world!"

A common amplification of this statement is "I will be different from you, Mom," by the daughter, and "I will be different from you, Dad," by the son. While perhaps not communicated orally, this declaration of independence is nonetheless made in one form or another.

The third major identity statement occurs for most people somewhere in their 40s and is a poignant, reality-loaded response to young adults' seemingly boundless enthusiasm: "I am limited. I wasn't as successful as I said I'd be. I didn't become President, I'm not going to have that home on the lake." Recognition of limitations, while frustrating and sometimes hard to swallow, is necessary if the person is to deal positively with the aging process. For then, she can assess realistically where she is and where she wants to go next. She can set new goals and priorities and take advantage of new opportunities.

And that is really what the aging process is about: handling the issues and stresses of each stage in our growth and development so we can move on to the next.

Remember that old cliché, "Life is one darn thing after another?" Actually, the wag who gave that pearl to us, knew what she was talking about.

Now for you older folks who are wondering what the fourth stage is about, I'm working on it. I already know that the word "procrastination" will be in there somewhere.

Defining our character

Remember what it was like to be a kid?

You might want to try!

Because who we are today, and what we do and find so objectionable or so wonderful is because of what we learned when we were young.

It's when our values were forming and when our likes and dislikes were developing.

It's when our character began to take shape.

And that, dear readers, is the topic of particular interest to me today.

If we say someone has "character," it calls to mind the qualities of integrity, honesty, respectability and goodness. We are likely describing a person of high ethical, moral behavior.

If we describe someone by saying, "He's quite a character!" we usually interpret it to mean the recipient is unique, strange, peculiar, odd, eccentric, unconventional, or maybe even daft.

In other words, that person hears bells the rest of us don't hear and marches to drummers when the rest of us are listening to flutes.

Each of us has a character that results from the life we have led. We have been molded by our experiences and our responses to them.

As children, we encountered a world we could scarcely comprehend. If we were lucky, our parents coached us through the rough spots that caused us pain and suffering.

Schools helped mold our character. Some of us left more self-confident while others of us emerged insecure, distrusting our abilities. All of us learned things that benefited us, things that didn't and things that made us who we are today.

Most of us became husbands and wives. We discovered how joyous and difficult it is to live intimately with another human being.

We learned to compromise, tested our coping skills, determined that we needed to be adaptable and less selfish and realized that giving and receiving love were more complex than our juvenile concepts prepared us for.

Many of us became parents, little comprehending what we had gotten ourselves into. Becoming one was easy; being one was challenging. It was in this role that we began to understand the meaning of sacrifice, for no matter how well we had prepared none of us could conceive of what we would have to give up to become a responsible mother or father. Nor could we anticipate the serendipitous joys inherent in parenting roles either.

These experiences and many more made us who we are today.

Along the way, there have been bumps, hard knocks, wearying problems and stressful fears, which have taken their toll. Some of us have had to correct serious flaws before we could begin dealing with life in positive, constructive ways. Others of us are still reeling from reverses and need to reach out for help.

For those of us in our later years, it's our character that serves as a guide for whatever comes.

By now our character is well formed. Who we are today is who we will likely be tomorrow. We have been tempered and toughened by time.

That's as it should be, for each of us will have to face and deal with major losses—of loved ones, friends, health, as well as the ultimate loss of life itself.

Our character will be severely tested.

As the final chapter is completed, the history we leave is how our character performed and prevailed against the challenging circumstances we encountered in life.

And how we met the final challenges life presented us.

Rationalizations

I watched an interview recently of an athlete. He reminded me of an old tennis rival I used to compete against. He always had an excuse for his loss. He wasn't feeling well. He had a new racquet that didn't feel right. The strings were too loose.

Then there was a friend of mine who didn't get the job she applied for. "I didn't want it anyhow. It would have meant more work."

I could have asked her why she applied, but I didn't.

What each of these persons told me was convincing and logical — to them.

What I heard both times was rationalization.

Most of us are pretty good at recognizing rationalizations, except when we're using them.

Rationalizations explain our behavior in ways that protect us from facing the truth about ourselves. Our rationalizations make sense to us.

"I didn't get the promotion because I don't have a college degree," was an explanation given by a man who had been told by his boss that he lacked leadership qualities and did not get along well with his colleagues.

Was this man lying? Not deliberately. Rather, he was using a flawed explanation to hide from himself painful or unpleasant facts. Since he could not accept the real reason for not being promoted, he devised an explanation that excused his being passed over that didn't reflect negatively on him.

Rationalization is also commonly used when people try to justify their prejudices. "I would have shown the Wilsons that house, but I knew they wouldn't be comfortable in that neighborhood." To the Realtor, this explanation justifies his reason for not showing a black family a home in the white section of town.

"She's a good worker but Tom has a family to support." So Tom gets the promotion instead of Doris, even though his performance appraisals have shown fewer desirable work habits and less creativity.

Some people use rationalizations to relieve themselves of responsibility for their behavior. "If I hadn't been interrupted so much, I wouldn't have made those errors." "If Jamie wasn't always pestering me, I wouldn't have burned those steaks."

In organizations, rationalizations are often used by people who find it difficult to adapt to change. Here's an example: when a new computer system was installed in a business corporation, employees were encouraged to attend an in-service training course to learn how to use it. Those who qualified would have their jobs reclassified and receive a substantial pay raise. Only a handful of employees signed up. Most said they were too busy while others indicated that the old system was preferable to the new one. None acknowledged their fears that they might be unable to learn the new system or to learn as quickly as others.

Fear of change and lack of confidence in one's ability to learn new ways frequently produce rationalizations. It is difficult for an employee to say to his or her boss, "I don't like change," or "I'm afraid I won't be able to handle the system."

What can we do about our rationalizations? Try to be honest with ourselves and recognize when we are using one. Then try to understand why we are fearful and self-protective in a particular situation.

And whenever we think our response to something someone says or does is a rationalization, ask your spouse or a good friend for an outside opinion.

Remember, we may not be sure, but chances are, they will be.

We all do it

Here I am in my 85th year and I'm still doing it!
It's how I spend most of each day.
I could worry about it, but what the heck, everybody does it.
We talk to ourselves day in, day out.
Fortunately, I have the good sense to keep most of that stuff to myself. Almost all of it would be really boring, even to my best friends.

But when I recall how I used to talk to myself when I was young, I didn't have this perspective. My small talk was, essentially, my identity— my real self. At least I thought so back then.

I recollect magnifying almost everything. "I'm so small. The girls in my class treat me like their kid brother. I'll never get a date."

"If I don't get picked for the team, I'm worthless."

"Everyone is better at algebra then I am."

Obviously, a critical characteristic of my self-talk was negativism. I was so unsure of myself, struggling to discover an identity, and pretty certain that all the other kids had their acts together.

They didn't, of course, but it took me a few more years to figure that out. When you're a self-centered, wobbly, budding adolescent, your impressions of other people aren't very accurate.

As a young adult I came to understand that I was solely responsible for writing my own script. Parents and friends could be contributors, but I had the responsibility.

I gradually learned that the way we talk to ourselves is especially revealing and meaningful since it discloses our inner-most feelings and responses to what is going on in our lives.

Through the years I've learned some lessons from my self-talk that not only alert me to what's really happening in my life, but enable me to cope better as well.

For instance, when I start to overgeneralize—"If I don't do well in this, I won't do anything else well either"—I caution myself to be more realistic.

When I revert to negative self-talk—"I can't write a good column on this topic, so there is no use trying"—I try to pull myself together with positive thoughts.

When my self-talk becomes egocentric—"Since she is in a rotten mood today, it must be because of something I've done"—I have to remind myself that I am not necessarily responsible for other person's moods or feelings.

167

When I let myself be governed by "shoulds"—"I should be smarter, I should have picked up on what she really said, I should have done this or that"—I step back to remind myself that "shoulds" produce guilt and I don't need any more of that.

Realizing that what I say to myself can be stressful and dangerous to my health, I need to monitor my self-talk more carefully. What I think affects the way I feel. If I am unhappy, I need to look in myself for the reason.

I need to offset exaggerated, negative thinking with reality checks. Thankfully, My Beloved and friends often help me gain a sense of perspective.

And if I don't like the way I'm feeling or the way things are going in my life, I know that I probably need to change the way I'm talking about myself.

Self-talk. We all do it.

Let's try to keep it as positive as we can.

Reasonable

"Be reasonable."

"Me?" I'm always reasonable. It's you who isn't being reasonable."

"You don't make sense."

"Well, you aren't logical."

Ever said anything like this? Or been accused of being unreasonable, nonsensical or illogical?

Probably.

Aristotle defined MAN as "the reasoning animal." That sounds reasonable. The problem is, if we're so reasonable, why do we argue or differ so much?

Why is it you and I can look at the same facts and reach different conclusions?

On a college campus, a number of women students were being assaulted. The college president called in her deans to discuss what should be done.

"We simply can't sit by and do nothing," she said.

"Why don't we initiate a curfew?" suggested the Dean of Men. "If the women are confined to their dorms, the problem will be solved."

That sounded logical to most of those in the room, until the Dean of Women said, "The problem is not the women. It's the men. If there is to be a curfew, the men should be confined to their dorms, not the women."

Know what a syllogism is?

It's a form of reasoning in which two statements or premises are made from which a logical conclusion is drawn. One of the most famous is Aristotle's: "All men are mortal. Socrates is a man. Therefore, Socrates is mortal."

Sound simple, doesn't it? If we all followed this formula and made statements or carried on arguments in this manner, misunderstandings and disagreements should diminish, right?

Unfortunately, most of us frequently omit a premise or conclusion, or communicate a false premise or conclusion.

Let's try a couple of examples: "Good fathers don't yell at their kids. I yelled at mine. Therefore, I was not a good father."

A politician says, "I schedule regular meetings for citizens so I can listen to their complaints. Few people attend. Therefore, the citizens must be happy with the job I am doing."

A common error in arguments or statements is to state "A is B," when actually "some A is B." This is a basis of prejudiced statements, which

169

lumps individuals and groups into sweeping generalized stereotypes. Whenever an argument implies "all" are involved, check quickly to see if "some" is a more accurate statement.

Keep in mind that syllogisms have four possible combinations: premises may be true and the conclusions false, the premises false and the conclusions true, or both the premises and conclusion may be true—or false.

And watch for statistical falsehoods: "Joe smoked six packs of cigarettes a day. He smoked for sixty years. Therefore, smoking can't be harmful to your health." When evidence is statistical, a few contrary examples do not disprove the data.

Logical, reasonable thinking.

It may be rare, but it's worth shooting for!

Labels

It's a sad commentary, but I believe we the people are addicted to labels.

I'm not referring to Dior, Gucci, Sara Lee, or Pepsi.

Of far more concern to me is our simplistic labeling of organizations, groups and individuals. "All Muslims are…" "All women are…" "All Republicans are…" "All liberals are…" And so on!

Labeling means we no longer have to deal with people as individuals. Simplification denies individuality and lumps together those who may possess a few characteristics and minor involvement with an organization with those who have major commitments or identification. The labeled become victims of the labeler. Not only does labeling often reveal the ignorance of the labeler—along with a lack of imagination and vocabulary—but it often smacks of childish name-calling.

You and I are complex individuals. In no way are we simple or easily described. You and I are far more than a conservative or a Democrat or a Native American. Each of us is a complicated, perplexing, variegated puzzle. In other words—an enigmatic human being.

Politicians—especially when running for public office—rely on labels. Particularly negative ones. Reason, honesty, good sense, civility, respect, accuracy, truth and other admirable personal qualities are largely absent from the public speeches of candidates. Scurrilous attacks prevail; character assassination is apparently acceptable if not the required mode of discourse.

Personal labeling is one of the major paths to bigotry and prejudice. Painting individuals and groups with inaccurate and oversimplified generalizations does harm not just to the accused but to the accuser as well. The character of the labeler is clearly besmirched and damaged.

But there is another level of labeling that yanks my chain—those used on mentally disturbed individuals.

I can think of no good reason to hang labels such as paranoid, schizophrenic or manic-depressive on people. They frighten the patients and relatives, raise doubts that the person is curable, and are such depressing labels that they convey gloom rather than hope.

But that's not all. Labels of this nature tend to become self-fulfilling; treat people as schizophrenic and it's likely they will behave as schizophrenic Label a person and we tend to relate to the label, not the person. Labeling may be appropriate for some statistical chart, but has nothing to do with effective treatment.

171

As the late psychiatrist Dr. Karl Menninger wrote, "We must view mental illness as simply a considerable degree of disorganization in a particular person. And we must find ways of improving his organization."

He goes on to discuss his opposition to labeling: "It hurts the individual. The individual so labeled is no longer a troubled individual. He's no longer just a sick man or a patient. He is regarded now as belonging to a special class of people to be treated, perhaps to be feared, to be scorned, to be pitied, to be avoided—always to be degraded, always to be suspect in regard to his predictability, in regard to his adaptability, and in regard to his competence. Objectively and subjectively he is stigmatized even if he ceases to have any of the symptoms upon which the original labeling was established."

The fact is, one person's illness is different from another person's, no matter how similar the symptoms.

And that's the point. Each of us is an original. Labeling is a sterile and dehumanizing way of looking at a person or a group. In our own way, each of us is an exception to any label.

Finally, if you have grown weary of all of the name-calling and shallow labeling by presidential candidates and editorial writers, you may wish to read a personality profile of Mr. Trump written by a psychologist. Don P. McAdams is the Henry Wade Rogers Professor of Psychology and the director of the Foley Center for the Study of Lives at Northwestern University.

The commentary is titled "The Mind of Donald Trump" and is the feature article in this month's (June) Atlantic magazine.

What is happiness?

When I was young, I thought I knew what happiness was.

It was recess. It was spring. It was playing with my dog, Wolf. It was sitting in a cool movie theater during the summer. It was swimming in a nearby lake.

Now, as an adult, I'm not so sure what happiness is.

Somehow in the process of growing up it got complicated.

I read John Stuart Mill. "Ask yourself whether you are happy, and you cease to be so." Then he wrote, "…Happiness cannot be pursued; it must ensue, as the unintended side-effect of one's personal dedication to a course greater than oneself."

That doesn't sound simple to me!

So I began looking at adults I knew who were happy and those who weren't and I started reading books about happiness.

Here is what I now think I know.

Why do people yearn for happiness so desperately, yet fail to find it?

Certainly one answer is that they are looking in the wrong places.

Some folks believe that money will lead them to it. Others are convinced that power is the answer.

However, there is considerable evidence that happiness doesn't occur because of fortunes or actions.

I read a book by Mihaly Csikszentmihalyi titled "FLOW: The Psychology of Optimal Experience." He wrote this about happiness: "It does not depend on outside events, but, rather, on how we interpret them. Happiness, in fact, is a condition that must be prepared for, cultivated, and defended privately by each person. People who learn to control inner experience will be able to determine the quality of their lives, which is as close as any of us can come to being happy."

Okay, so we might not be able to achieve happiness by consciously searching for it.

So we begin by deciding what parts of our lives we can and cannot control. Most of the forces impacting on our lives are outside of our control—intelligence, looks, temperament, when we were born, who are parents were, whether there will be war, the economic situation, who will be the next president, which party will control congress.

It seems pretty clear to me that we live in a world where outside forces greatly influence—and sometimes govern—who we are and what we do.

But, even when buffeted by an enormous number of external forces, most of us have experienced times when we have felt in control and on top of things.

Listen again to Mihaly C. "Contrary to what we usually believe, the best moments in our lives are not the passive, receptive, relaxing times, although such experiences can also be enjoyable if we have worked hard to attain them. The best moments usually occur when a person's body or mind is stretched to its limits in a voluntary effort to accomplish something difficult and worthwhile."

He calls these moments or times when we feel in control of our actions, "optimal experiences." He goes on to tell us that, "Getting control of life is never easy, and sometimes it can be definitely painful. But in the long run, optimal experiences add up to a sense of mastery—or perhaps better, a sense of participation in determining the content of life—that comes as close to what is usually meant by happiness as anything else we can conceivably imagine."

What Mr. C is describing is a state in which we are so involved in an activity that nothing else seems to matter. What we are doing is so enjoyable that all else happening around us is beyond our consciousness.

The message? Control your inner life and happiness will likely result. And your happiest times will be when you are doing and enjoying something for its own sake, whether its sports, games, hobbies, work, family, volunteer activities, reading, hiking, writing, gardening, or working on a project.

You cannot achieve happiness when you are so fixated on what you want to achieve that you cease to derive pleasure from what you are doing at the moment.

Happiness, then, is within each of us.

We have been grievously misled if we believe it is somewhere "out there" waiting to be found.

Whew! That's enough for now. I'm going to recess!

P.S. Happiness is also not having to spell Mijhaly's last name ever again!

Memories

Reading a recent article about the high percentage of veterans committing suicide and the many who are struggling with PTSD (Post Traumatic Stress Disorder) provoked a memory that took me back to an important lesson I learned sixty-three years ago when I was serving a tour of duty with the U.S. Army in Korea.

After a truce was reached in the summer of 1953, our unit handled the repatriation of prisoners. We returned North Koreans and Chinese to Panmunjom and welcomed young men back from the NK prison camps. Interviewing the former POW's was a major learning experience.

The stories they told us about the treatment they received from their captors were deeply disturbing.

The years since have little diminished the impact of those encounters. It is still painful to recall the debriefings, which gives me a good idea how former POWs of later wars must feel.

One lesson of that ordeal became clear during a conversation with an old acquaintance—he didn't live in the Prescott area—who was well into major health consciousness. He worked out daily, ate healthy foods and prided himself on "looking good."

The fact is, he did look good!

So, why was I uneasy about our conversation? And why did my mind transfer itself from him back to Korea?

It was because I perceived that this man equated his body with himself. He believed that how he looked determined who he is. My assessment of him was quite different. To my way of thinking, he was quite healthy physically, but was not living a healthy life.

You see, reflecting on conversations with many POWs years ago whose bodies were not healthy still persuades me that the very essence of them was alive, dynamic and healthy. They talked about how they kept their minds alive while living in captivity, of goals they intended to pursue, how their values and beliefs saw them through the toughest times, and why their spirits overcame the weakness of their bodies. In the worst of times, they called on resources other than their crippled bodies to sustain and empower them.

In thinking about them, it appears to me that people with physically sound bodies whose lives lack direction and purpose may not be healthy, while people whose bodies are sick or even crippled can lead lives of great meaning.

The old acquaintance of mine was most attractive on the outside, but badly flawed inside.

A healthy person is defined as much by her or his thoughts and feelings as by flesh and bones. A healthy body is better seen as a means, not an end. It can be used to live in a meaningful, rich way or it can be a vehicle which leads a person to despair.

Put differently, the POWs I remember best were above all else, survivors. They survived being victimized. They were able to transform themselves from being victims of the worst kind of physical and psychological torture to seeing themselves as survivors.

In the most degrading and horrible physical conditions, they possessed a courage and strength which became an effective antidote to their badly weakened bodies.

One doesn't forget statements like, "I knew I couldn't give in to them." "I wouldn't permit myself to give up hope." Or the one that made the biggest impression on this 22 year-old. "I had too much to live for to let them get to me."

It was a profound and moving lesson in inner strength.

It was also a profound lesson in outer strength.

When the latter was taken away, the former sustained them.

I concluded that the former was more important. Not that one shouldn't exercise and eat healthy foods. But nourishing the inner self requires equally diligent attention.

Want to undertake your own exploration of the subject of inner resources? A good source is the book, The Human Patient, by Naomi Remen, M.D.

A note from the teacher

(It won't happen, but I suspect as a new school year begins that a number of teachers would like to send a note home to parents that would go something like this.)

Dear Parent:

As you son's elementary school teacher, I pledge to do my best to see that his year in my class is beneficial and challenging to him.

However, while I commit myself to making his learning experience memorable and rewarding, I have expectations of you as well. I intend to fulfill my responsibilities to your son, and expect you to do the same. Only if we work together will he grow and develop as we want him to. Therefore, I expect the following from you as a parent:

• Accept your share of responsibility for your son's education. Since you interact together daily, you have far more influence over what your son learns than I do. His education is primarily in your hands. I've got him for a few hours a day and for nine months; you've got him for his entire childhood. I'm no miracle-worker. I can't undo what you have done.

• To do my job well, I need your support. If I call you, respond. If I ask you to come talk to me, come. If I send homework home, see that he does it. When there are school functions, be here. If you have some extra time, volunteer to help our school. You and I are in this together—don't ever forget that!

• The environment you create at home for your son is infinitely more important than the one I create in the classroom. Try hard to be the very best parent you can be. Talk to your son about his school day, praise him, and let him know every day that you care about him and what he is doing. I teach because I like kids; I hope you are a parent for the same reason.

• Read to and with your son. You can't raise a reader if reading is not an important part of family life. Restrict the time he watches TV as well as the quality of the programs. Ditto with his I-Pad if he has one. Don't use TV as a substitute for child care. I want an engaged, active learner in my class, not a kid who sits passively in front of me waiting to be entertained.

• Be a good listener. Your son will respond positively to you if you are. When he speaks, listen to what he has to say. Similarly, if I call to talk with you, listen up. I am at least as busy as you are, so when I call to speak about your son, pay attention!

• Give your son a clear structure for his life. Let him know what he can and can't do. He needs a firm hand and consistent discipline. But never let that hand land on him. I want children in my class who are not

177

frightened by adults, abused by parents, or scared of being whipped by the teacher.

• Whether you like it or not, you are his role model. Who you are and what you do are more important than what you say to him. Be the best role model you can be. If you've got problems that prevent you from being a good parent, get help.

• Tell your son that you love him and have confidence in him. He needs to hear both—regularly. Expect much from him and you will likely get it—so long as it is couched in love. Each night when he gets in bed, the last words he should hear are, I love you! You do this for him, and I'll love you too!

Sincerely,
His Teacher

The Barbershop

It was never known as just the neighborhood barbershop.

It was Henry's. He was the resident dispenser of wisdom for the entire block of stores that made up a section of Kansas City's 39th Street. His two-chair shop was distinguished by the obligatory red and white revolving cylinder, but that particular identification was unnecessary. Men knew that Henry's was next to the saloon and we kids knew it was next to the candy store.

Henry's was smack in the middle of the best of both worlds, at least according to the prescribed masculine mode of thinking.

As Henry himself repeated, "I've got the choice location in town."

While most of my buddies detested haircuts, I secretly looked forward to them. On Saturday mornings, Dad and I would wait for our turns while listening to Henry and the other regulars discuss "the world news." It was from Henry that I learned war was coming.

"Roosevelt will get us into it, mark my words," Henry would affirm at least once every hour. "Then you'll have to go, Fred, and so will you, Marvin, and so will my son back in Cleveland. You and I are too old, Roy," he said to my father. "And the squirt's too young."

I already figured I wasn't old enough to fight. After all, I was still sitting on the board Henry placed across the arms of the barber chair. But I was sure glad to hear him say Dad was too old to go.

Several months later what Henry predicted came true. Fred and Marvin went off to war. After that I paid even more attention to what Henry said.

It wasn't much later that Louie the barber came to work for Henry. He had already been in the fighting and had a leg that wouldn't bend. All of us regulars took our time trusting him with the scissors. When his chair was empty, we'd tell him we were waiting for Henry.

One Saturday, after scrutinizing me for several minutes, Henry told me I would look good with a crewcut. He said that all the marines were getting them and that I ought to be first in the neighborhood to have one. I knew old Henry wouldn't steer me wrong, so I responded, "Sure!" It was only then that he told me Louie was the expert on crewcuts. It was too late to back down.

Without question, that was the longest haircut of my life. His clippers never stopped. As my hair covered the floor, I noticed Henry kept smiling at me. When it was over I felt naked, but relieved I still had two ears. But again, Henry knew what he was doing, because within a week, most of my buddies got crewcuts from Louie, so I felt relieved. I suspect Louie did too.

Sometime during the fall of 1944, when Dad and I went for our haircuts, we discovered Henry wasn't there. That had never happened before. "Where's Henry?" Dad asked.

"His son was killed in action," Louie replied. "He's taking a few days off."

It was two Saturday's later that we saw Henry again. He looked sick and distracted, and I didn't know what to say to him, but Dad did. They talked quietly while he cut Dad's hair. I couldn't hear their conversation because Louie kept the clippers busy on me, but I did see Henry wipe tears away a couple of times.

After that Saturday it seemed like Henry's place smelled less of lilac cologne and hair tonic and more like the smell that seeped out of the saloon door. Dad said that Henry was spending more time on breaks than he was cutting hair. I didn't understand much of what was going on, but I knew Henry wasn't looking too good.

Then one Saturday we walked into the shop and Louie was working first chair. Henry's chair.

"I'm buying Henry out," Louie told us. "He's decided to take things easier." After we left, Dad explained that because of his son's death, Henry's health had gone downhill.

I had grown to like Louie, but the shop was never the same without Henry.

I discovered it wasn't the same without Marvin either. He never came back from the war. I drifted away from Henry's and from the neighborhood for that matter. After the war ended, I spent more time attending high school functions several miles away, and made new friends who lived in other neighborhoods.

A part of my life ended.

But I never pass a barber poll without thinking of Henry's, and how important those Saturday mornings were to a boy growing up during World War II.

Inventors

We humans are born inventors.

And many of us did our best inventing when we were children. While some of us concocted boisterous games, wondrous kingdoms and glorious fairytales, other children imagined a gentle world in which parents didn't yell, fight or hit and where everyone in the family had enough food to eat every day of the week.

As we matured from children to youths, we may have found our inventive nature discouraged. We were instructed to conform to new, unexamined behavior patterns, often outdated in terms of need or purpose, created by parents and others who "knew best." While we yearned to invent, we were admonished to follow instructions, write to fit a designated mold, respond to questions with prescribed answers and treat people in the same way in which we observed our parents relating to others.

We learned there is an acceptable, approved way of doing, saying, even looking at things when adults are around.

We also learned that many adults were not really interested in our inventiveness. Growing up often meant relinquishing precious childhood worlds we imagined and leaving behind those creations that made our lives exciting. Adults communicated to us—in many ways—that we should "get down to business," which, we learned, didn't include the little fantasies our imaginations had created.

Most of us invented selves that conformed to what our parents wanted us to develop. We learned that who we were to become should not differ drastically from all those people who inhabited our immediate world. We were bracketed by admonitions to "follow the crowd, swim with the stream and do in Rome as the Romans do." Adapting, accommodating, reconciling, assimilating and compromising became more than words as we entered the adult world.

For many of us the self we invented was designed to be safe, conforming and—sad to say—inconsequential. To get ahead, we learned "to get along." We became rational, utilitarian, pragmatic, efficient and—dull. We convinced ourselves that as adults we must put behind us our frivolous, spirited, merry child-like games and behave in mature, prudent and sensible ways.

Then there were some of us who invented nasty, mean-spirited selves. Others invented self-righteous, egocentric selves. And there were those who developed glib, superficial selves to hide their insecurities.

Yet, many of us continued to dream and in those dreams we recreated and reinvented ourselves in ways that ennobled us. We explored paths that led to enlightenment, illumination and excitement. We became different individuals than who we used to be. Not totally, of course, but at least enough to give us inner satisfaction and enable us to enjoy the changes.

Of course, none of us reinvented ourselves alone. Our families and friends, along with the many, varied forces we encountered throughout our lives helped shape our redevelopment. And if we were lucky, we had teachers who taught us to improvise, and encouraged us to nurture our inventive spirit and develop imaginative approaches to problems and challenges.

And there were those precious teachers who encouraged us to dream. We shall never forget them.

The fact is, each of us is, to some degree, still a dreamer, still an inventor.

There is the hope that no matter our age our innate inventive spirit will be nurtured and rekindled; that some of those childhood dreams will become real again.

Henry David Thoreau wrote: "I have learned this at least by my experiment: that if one advances confidently in the direction of his dreams, and endeavors to lead that life which he has imagined, he will meet with a success unexpected in common hours."

Imagination is common to inventors.

And that still means all of us!

The sixth sense

How superstitious are you?

Do you believe in supernatural experiences?

One accepted definition of superstition is belief in the supernatural. However, what is superstitious in one society may not be in another. Further, there are degrees of superstition. You may believe in luck, but not in the supernatural.

Perhaps a more useful definition of superstition is that it is any set of beliefs that endure through time and are not adequately supported by facts.

Hunches are short term superstitions.

And all of us rely on them.

Which explains why we have irrational tendencies. Obviously, some of us have more than others. But all of us respond to promptings from within that are separate from the five senses of touch, hearing, sight, sound and taste.

Some people, including scientists, call these inner forces, "the sixth sense." Primitive forms of life, they tell us, relied on this sense, which involves something we now call instinct. As the human animal evolved, development of the other senses began to replace instinct. When, as a species, we began to develop the power of reasoning, the instinctual sense diminished.

But instinct still operates and guides us—sometimes as much, if not more, than our other senses. Its importance in our lives is largely determined by how we regard it. If I place a high value on my hunches, or what some call intuition, I am likely to give my sixth sense the kind of attention I do my other senses.

In my case, while I indeed rely on my eyes to see things, I also rely on my "mind's eye" to "see" things as well. I pay attention to my dreams and visions when there is no actual "sight."

Let's carry this line of thinking a step further. A number of institutions of higher learning along with psychical research centers around the world are busy exploring the field of the paranormal (or supernatural). They regard such studies as appropriate for academic exploration because they are a means of enlarging and better understanding the human experience.

Opposed to these studies are those who embrace materialism—the idea that that there is no such thing as the supernatural. Materialists discount research into this field and consign persons who believe in it, or pursue it as a legitimate object for study, as kooks, frauds or at best, misguided.

183

However, among those who have examined supernatural incidents and paranormal phenomena and are familiar with the wide body of research in this field, there are those who believe that the spirit world is as real as the one they walk around in.

Most of us have used our extra sensory perception ability when we have a hunch, or felt impelled to do something or not do it or when we felt visited by someone not physically present.

Some investigators believe that around half the population, at least, have had dreams or visions that later came to pass.

There is no doubt that all of us have perceptions beyond the five physical senses.

The challenge is to tune into them if you haven't already, and expand your sixth sense in order to take full advantage of the powers within available to you.

If you are curious how to do this, or are simply interested in learning more about the research and studies in this fascinating field, head for the section of the Prescott Public Library under the classification number 130.

Friendship

It's happening more frequently now.

I understand it's a result of age, but it doesn't make it any easier.

In this case, the man who walked into the mist was a friend from my early life in Kansas City, my best friend during our final two years of high school.

We were in band together for four years, and both of us were starters on the city championship basketball team. He was 6-foot-5 inches tall. I was not.

When I left for college, he organized a small group of my friends and they all came to the bus station to see me off. I went to college in Virginia and he attended nearby Kansas University. During those years we saw less and less of each other, but the friendship continued.

Two years of army service extended the separation, then graduate school and subsequent career moves around the country completed the fracture. Only three times did we manage to meet during those many years.

Now we have no more chances to be together. The opportunities are gone, squandered. That's what is especially painful.

Which is why the following anonymous poem has such meaning to me—and perhaps to you as well.

Around the corner I have a friend
In this great city that has no end.
Yet days go by and weeks rush on,
And before I know it a year has gone.
And I never see my old friend's face,
For life's a swift and terrible race.
He knows I like him just as well,
As in the days I rang his bell.
And he rang mine, we were younger then.
And now we are busy, tired men.
Tired of playing a foolish game.
Tired of trying to make a name.
"Tomorrow" I say, I will call on him."
But tomorrow comes and tomorrow goes,
And the distance between us grows and grows.
Around the corner, yet miles away.
Here's a telegram, Jim died today.
And that's what I get and deserve in the end.
Around the corner I had a friend.

The young couple

How strange they sometimes are.

I was waiting for the traffic light at a corner of the Prescott Plaza when I saw an elderly couple sitting on a bench holding hands. They were looking at each other with loving smiles; both seemed to be in a state of utter contentment.

As the light changed and I drove across the intersection, a long-buried memory captured my attention, and a story I thought I had forgotten came back into my consciousness.

As near as I can recall, the event occurred in the spring of 1942. Overlooking a nearby large park was a limestone outcropping of rock which gave those of us who knew about it an impressive view of central Kansas City, Mo.

I loved that cliff. Sometimes friends and I would hike through the woods to picnic on it, but most of the time I would go alone. It became sort of a sanctuary for me, although at age 11, I had no idea my rock could be associated with such a big word.

It was early one Saturday morning when I hiked to it, eager to look at the beautiful rain clouds circling the city. Approaching through a small forest, I was surprised to see a young couple standing on the rock. Until then, I thought only my friends and I knew about it. Since I was too shy to walk out on the cliff where they would see me, I crouched behind a large clump of bushes, curious about who they were, but more eager for them to leave.

For several minutes they held hands, then put their arms around each other. They didn't kiss, just held each other tight. They talked quietly for a 5 or 10 minutes, then left.

A month or two later, when several of us guys went to the cliff, we saw the woman there alone. She was just sitting, staring out over the city. After a while, she got up and left.

I didn't see her again until the next fall. School had started and I sometimes detoured to the cliff on my way home. I was near the tip of the rock when I saw her. We were both startled. I think I muttered something about not meaning to scare her and she said she wasn't and that I had as much right to be there as she did.

What I remember was that she was very pretty, maybe in her early twenties. She didn't look like a teenager and she wore a beautiful, small silver chain around her neck. I'd never seen one before so I asked her about it.

187

"My husband gave it to me before he left."

"Well, it's really pretty," I stammered before saying goodbye.

I told my mom about her being on the cliff and how I'd seen her there before with her husband. She told me he was likely in the Service since all the young men were.

Although I went to the cliff a number of times during the winter, I didn't see her again until just before school was out. Bobby Cox and I hiked there to eat our apples, as I recall. She was standing on the edge of the cliff crying. Neither of us knew what to do so we just watched her.

She stood there for a while, then slowly walked back through the woods to the street. We followed and saw her enter a small house that had a ramp going up the stairs to the front porch.

It was a few weeks later, while walking past the house with the ramp, that I saw her and her husband. They were sitting on the porch. He was in a wheelchair with a blanket over his legs. I thought that was strange because it was summer and it was hot.

When I told my mother about seeing them, she explained that he had lost one leg and most of the other one in the fighting. My first thought was that he would never be able to go out to the cliff again because the woods were too thick and rocky for his wheelchair.

Looking back, I know the story isn't unusual for the war years, but it was my first real contact with what the fighting meant. Their lives had been changed forever.

In a small way, mine had too.

I continued to hike over to the cliff, but never did so without thinking of her—and them.

I hope the years since 1943 have been happy ones for them both.

On being pretty good

For years, My Beloved and I watched CBS on Sunday mornings because of Charles Kuralt. When he retired, we switched allegiance to his replacement, Charles Osgood. Now, he has retired. We think he merits an appropriate send-off. So, out of my files I found one of his poems. I hope you'll appreciate it as much as we do.

There once was a pretty good student,
Who sat in a pretty good class
And was taught by a pretty good teacher,
Who always let pretty good pass.
He wasn't terrific at reading,
He wasn't a whiz-bang at math.
But for him education was leading
Straight down a pretty good path.
He didn't find school too exciting,
But he wanted to do pretty well,
And he did have some trouble with writing,
And nobody had taught him to spell.
When doing arithmetic problems,
Pretty good was regarded as fine,
Five plus five needn't always add up to ten,
A pretty good answer was nine.
The pretty good class that he sat in
Was part of a pretty good school.
And the student was not an exception,
On the contrary, he was the rule.
The pretty good school that he went to
Was there in a pretty good town.
And nobody there seemed to notice
He could not tell a verb from a noun.
The pretty good student in fact was
Part of a pretty good mob.
And the first time he knew what he lacked was
When he looked for a pretty good job.
It was then, when he sought a position,
He discovered that life could be tough.
And he soon had a sneaky suspicion
Pretty good might not be good enough.

The pretty good town in our story
Was part of a pretty good state,
Which had pretty good aspirations,
And prayed for a pretty good fate.
There once was a pretty good nation,
Pretty proud of the greatness it had,
Which learned much too late,
If you want to be great,
Pretty good is, in fact, pretty bad.

Significant life lessons

Along with pounds one of the things we accumulate as we age are lessons.

The older we become, the more lessons we have collected.

Some are good, some lousy, and some meaningful and important, like those Granddaddyisms I shared with our eldest grandson.

For me at this late stage in my life, I feel like it's time to summarize. And no better time than on a weekend when we are giving thanks for our many blessings.

So what are the most significant lessons I have learned over the past 86 years? I may well alter the list tomorrow, but today here are my selections. They are in no priority order. Perhaps you may want to think about your own list!

*Intelligence is no guarantee of wisdom nor does sensitivity mean I will be more compassionate toward others. Intent, purpose and commitment must be factored into these equations. I do believe compassion is more critical to my development as a human being than intelligence.

*Making choices, and living with them, is as critical to my quality of life as any other critical factor. Like you, I suspect, I have made some superior choices during the years and some that I wish I hadn't. I live with both kinds.

*One of the most valuable assets I possess in a sense of humor. Without it I might not have won the heart of My Beloved, nor would I have weathered as well as I have the inevitable crises and downers that have occurred through the years. While I laugh less than I did in the earlier years, I am more sensitive to and appreciative of whimsy, irony, comedy and buffoonery which I observe in the human condition.

*Attitude may not be the most significant thing in my life, but it's close. I know I see the world not as it is, but as I am. My perception of reality determines my perspectives on life. My attitude is at the root of my perceptions and perspectives.

*What I do not know is infinitely greater than the little I do know and this realization is not only the true source of humility but the reason why I embrace the goal of being an active life-long learner. I have indeed been fortunate to live with a person who has the same goal.

*The natural vulnerability of childhood was followed, in my case, by a determined attempt to wear, during adolescence and early adulthood, a mask of invulnerability. After these years of immaturity, I was fortunate to learn, with the help and understanding of others, that vulnerability means having the strength to acknowledge weaknesses, limitations, uncertainty and confusion. Acknowledging that I am a flawed, imperfect human being was a necessary step to seeking the forgiveness of others.

*There is more to life–and death – than we know. My experiences with the spirit world beyond physical death is one of the most important realities (and attitudes) I carry inside of me.

*It is important to live actively in the present. It is more challenging to do so now, in these later years, than when I was younger. There is a seductive pull of memories vying for attention with the real and compelling concerns for the here and now. Attending to the present is a significant challenge, but an exceedingly essential one.

*It has been critical to develop within me a special place which nourishes my spirit when the outer world seeks to disturb or torment me. My inner world is lively, comforting, supportive, astonishingly provocative, and is tuned frequently to the exploration of wonder and the nurture of curiosity.

*It has long been essential for me to believe in what Marian Wright Edelman calls the Fellowship of Human Beings. The principle of inclusion—not exclusion—of people different from me is critical to my attempt to become fully human. Healing and love are more sensible, humane and necessary for the survival of our earthly family than divisiveness and hatred.

*Finally, to love someone deeply, and be loved in return, is the greatest of personal blessings and the most important lesson I have learned. I am a very fortunate individual.

Okay, what are yours??

A life script

"Life handed me a lousy script."

"Give it back," I replied.

Her dumbfounded expression confirmed my belief that this alternative hadn't occurred to her.

"What do you mean, give it back? I've got to deal with the hand I've been dealt, don't I?"

"Of course not. You've got the power to develop a new script if you really want to."

This conversation, which occurred many years ago, began a counseling session with a bank executive who came to me to discuss her increasingly unhappy marriage and her dissatisfaction with life in general.

Many of us live by scripts that are unsuitable, or worse, dangerous. Each of us decides, consciously or unconsciously, to either live with our script, modify it, or change it significantly. Few of us need to live with one that is detrimental to our physical or psychological well-being. Most of us have the power to write a new one if we want to badly enough.

Of course, some people decide to live in ways that are unhealthy. Others enjoy a certain amount of suffering and pain. Then there are those who take perverse pleasure in blaming other people or circumstances for their unhappiness. Convincing themselves that they are not responsible for their actions or attitudes excuses them from accepting responsibility for their feelings. "I can't be blamed for my misfortune," is the script they live by.

Criticizing, reproaching, denouncing, accusing and finding fault with others beats holding oneself accountable for the way life is developing.

Other folks may, knowingly or unknowingly, adopt the beliefs and values of one or both their parents rather than form ones themselves. Sometimes that works and sometimes, not.

Developing one's own set of beliefs, attitudes and opinions requires effort, individual thinking and a willingness to explore ideas and topics critically with a certain degree of objectivity—a proactive step that is much tougher than simply assuming uncritically those of parents or friends.

While each of us is significantly influenced by parents, we need not be controlled by them. If what they believe causes us pain, suffering, marital conflict or forces us to run counter to laws or ethical/moral conduct, then we should reject their scripts and write our own.

One of the most memorable conversations I remember was with a friend whose five-year old son had drawn boldly with crayons on his bedroom wall. When confronted, the lad exclaimed that the "devil made me do it."

"Is the devil inside you?" his father asked.

"Yes," he replied.

"Then we don't want to feed him any ice cream or cake at your birthday party tomorrow, do we?"

It took the youngster several hours to figure out a response to that one. "The devil's gone, Daddy."

"He won't come back will he?"

"No."

From then on, the youngster pretty much wrote his own script.

It's good idea for all of us.

Odds & ends

• I am increasingly annoyed by the arrogance of certainty that has become pervasive in letters to the editors and in other communications. Righteous judgments that anoint individuals who disagree with those who "know" what is right and who is wrong seem on the rise. Labeling an individual as a liberal or conservative or a Democrat or Republican does not describe who he or she really is. Each of us is far more complicated. Let's pull the plug on anger and righteous judgments while elevating respect and love for one another.

• I believe we need to reaffirm that the world we live in is an interdependent community. The very real threat of global warming and human survival accentuates this reality. Old political beliefs based on power, acquisitions and economic/militaristic superiority deny reality. Planetary survival means that global leaders must recognize and champion policies that embrace the imperative of global connectedness. The human race is running out of time. The plundering of earth's resources must stop now!

• I fear that we — the human race — have elected to live by a set of values that is dehumanizing our lives. We have accepted a culture that has prioritized technology and material wealth while devaluing human life and the human spirit. Violence in our cities increases and reverence for life is increasingly undermined. Morality deteriorates as truth becomes less valued than wealth. Goodness, along with development of the human spirit, receives decreasing attention.

• I am disturbed that our fascination with and dependency on I-whatevers is rapidly diminishing the family time we are devoting to stories, rituals and ceremonies. Historically, stories, rituals and symbols have enabled children to appreciate the value of structure and to find meaning in their lives. One of the most important lessons young people need to learn is that structure equals support. Without structure, the love and care rendered by parents and elders is unlikely to be a determining factor in the development of a child. True love is always rooted in a caring family structure.

• Who we are, and who we become, is far more determined by what we feel than by what we know. If we build our lives around the virtues of love, hope and faith we are likely to live lives that are healthier and more fulfilling than if we choose to live life seeking intellectual certainties. It's not what we know that makes us healthy and happy, it's what we feel. What is in our hearts is far more important than what is in our heads.

195

• One of the most important lessons I learned years ago was that we see things not as they are, but as we are. It took me a few more years before I realized that I needed to add another perspective: I needed to learn to see things as they might be. I needed to "expand myself," and develop visions. I needed to develop dreams. The words of Dr. Hans Selye — the physician who took the word "stress" out of the physics lab and applied it to our behavior — became critical to my development. "Realistic people who pursue practical aims are rarely as realistic or practical in the long run of life, as the dreamers who pursue their dreams."

• The above perspective has led me to another important realization: to be wary of what I now think I know. What was an important truth to me yesterday may not be so important tomorrow. What made sense to me at one time in my life may not be what I can depend on today. Keeping an open mind is better than a closed one.

• I am at my best — as you are — when guided by reason, compassion and the transforming power of love.

Perfectionists

This is a column about perfectionists and imperfectionists.

There are way too many of the latter who think and behave as if they inhabit the bodies and minds of the former.

So you understand what I'm getting at, let me preface this small offering with the caveat that there are times and situations when I (and perhaps you) have needed the expertise of a perfectionist. Like the physician who repaired my heart, for instance.

But my history has been filled with too many folks who have made my days and years longer than necessary because they embrace a work or life pattern that has been carefully conditioned either by strong parental expectations or by their own deep-rooted commitment to the ideal of perfection.

The friend who had to give up his pursuit of becoming a tennis professional because he couldn't control his temper when he missed an easy shot. The lady who finally stopped writing a novel after several years because she simply couldn't "get it right" to her satisfaction.

They become locked into a life of considerable unhappiness, frustration and guilt.

It's when I meet or observe a person with this "impossible dream" that I silently rejoice in my acceptance of being an imperfectionist.

In fact, I am an enthusiastic, committed one.

I know that everything I do can be done better.

Every idea and thought can be improved on.

Everything I write can be rewritten in a more precise, concise, eloquent form.

Years ago I discovered I was a risk-taker. I like the challenge of breaking new ground, starting projects, taking first steps.

So I now feel comfortable producing columns and articles that may stimulate and provoke others to improve on them.

Of course, the more I submit my ideas to public scrutiny, the more chance there is I will be proved wrong or uninformed or illogical or just plain stupid.

But that's the risk each of us takes every time we act or make a decision. We subject ourselves to second guessing and criticism.

What each of us hopes for is understanding, tolerance, charity, and forgiveness.

In attempting to elevate the status of imperfection, am I condoning mediocrity, lesser effort and average performance?

Not at all. Being an imperfectionist doesn't mean that one doesn't attempt to exert his or her best effort. What it does mean is that we put forth as good an effort as possible, remaining realistic in our expectations.

"It won't be perfect, but it will be the best I can do at this time."

Sadly, too many people are being conditioned to think that it is possible to give a 110 percent effort.

Or that if we only try harder and longer, we can achieve a perfect marriage or play a perfect tennis match or be a perfect boss or write a perfect article.

Nonsense!

This thinking is potentially self-destructive and dangerous.

Who wants to spend their life trying to measure up to standards that cannot be met?

There are enough chances for failure and guilt in our lives without setting ourselves up for more.

So, let's consider the virtues of being imperfectionists and risk-takers who put themselves out there with the bravado of Popeye: "I am what I am and that's all that I am."

Thoughts on becoming a gentle man

He swaggered out of the Palace Bar, obviously pleased with himself.

He stood on the sidewalk, preening, flexed his overdeveloped muscles, made a couple of lewd comments to two passing, attractive women, looked around to see who was admiring his pose, then strutted down the street, adoringly validating his performance in each store window.

This self-absorbed young man had built his image and his body around the old-fashioned concept of hard and tough. And unless he is very lucky, he will probably go through life trying to maintain that fatuous affectation. He may never learn what real toughness is.

I couldn't help but wonder what happened to that gentle, tender little boy who once resided in that man. I suspect the answer is that he was scared away by older boys, or ridiculed by the macho admonitions of cohorts who urged him to be a "real man," or killed off by parents, bosses or others who wanted him to behave like their version of a hardened grown-up.

It may be too late for him to get in touch with that warm and sensitive part of himself that was such a joy for him and others to be with. The tender part of him likely oppressed under the tough, arrogant, pseudo-manly exterior.

And in his present posture I doubt that he will ever have the opportunity to appreciate the words of St. Francis: "Nothing is so strong as gentleness. Nothing so gentle as real strength."

Nor will he likely understand that his carefully contrived armor of toughness is not strength. He has coated himself with a hard protective shell, within which, I suspect, is hollowness. He has paid attention to the outer man and neglected the inner one.

What I must hope for him, however, is that he somehow learns that strong people are not necessarily the toughest, loudest or biggest. Those characteristics may qualify them to be bullies, but little more. A person's strength is not worn on the outside but lives and moves within. Phony poses don't represent toughness; it's an inner quality.

Real strength can be soft, requiring the kind of toughness only a strong person can give. Real strength can't be built in a gym or owned like a pair of boots. It is a quality, however, that can be unlocked. It is not something to be controlled, but guided.

Being gentle with one's self and tender toward others is, perhaps, the most effective way of releasing one's inner strength. It means, for a male, uncovering the soft, caring, sensitive warm power within that frees him to

199

relate to himself in the fullness of his being. Using only half of his self—the self-defined macho elements—severely limits his emotional range.

Can this person develop a new set of values? He can if he realizes his life is out of proportion. He can if he understands that he will not be protected by his version of toughness, only by his humanity. In his present lifestyle his self-image will likely only relate to others who harbor the same self-concept which circumscribes his world to relatively few.

Perhaps he will learn that it will be his gentleness and tenderness that will make others want to be with him.

I hope he learns to become a gentle man.

Thoughts for Sunday morning

Among my favorite books in our library are those written by Dietrich Bonhoeffer. I never tire of re-reading them.

He was one of the most influential Christian theologians in the world.

So pervasive is his influence that church historian Martin Marty once suggested dividing the theological world into two groups: those who admit their debt to Bonhoeffer and those who borrow his ideas without acknowledgment.

Bonhoeffer was born in Breslau in 1906. Educated in Germany and the U.S., he early earned a reputation as a brilliant theologian. During World War II, he was imprisoned for resistance activities against the German government. For his part in a plot to kill Hitler, he was executed at Flossenburg concentration camp on April 9, 1945, a few days before it was liberated by allied troops.

Of his writings, the most impressive to me is The Cost of Discipleship. In this monumentally important book, Bonhoeffer discusses the difference between cheap and costly grace.

In theological terms, grace is understood as the free and unmerited love and favor of God. Bonhoeffer argues that churches are giving away grace at too low a cost. "Cheap grace is the grace we bestow on ourselves — the preaching of forgiveness without requiring repentance, baptism without church discipline. Cheap grace is grace without discipleship."

He argues that cheap grace is disastrous to our spiritual lives. Instead of pursuing a life that requires discipline, obedience and sacrifice, we accept a deceptive gospel that makes us feel strong when, in fact, we are weak and misguided. Instead of opening up our lives to Christ it (cheap grace) has closed it. Instead of calling us to follow Christ, it has hardened us in our disobedience.

For Bonhoeffer, "Costly grace is the gospel that must be sought again and again, the gift that must be asked for, the door at which a man must knock. It is costly because it causes us to follow...and because it costs a man his life. It is grace because it gives a man the only true life."

Perhaps the concept of costly grace can be understood by recounting a small part of Bonhoeffer's life. In June 1939, American friends got him out of Germany. Soon, however, it became clear to them that Bonhoeffer could and would not remain with them. His heart belonged to the German people who were suffering oppression and persecution under Hitler's policies.

Since he felt he could not desert them at a time when they needed him most, he returned to Germany.

Before leaving the U.S., Bonhoeffer wrote to his colleague, Reinhold Niebuhr, these words: "I shall have no right to participate in the reconstruction of Christian life in Germany after the war if I do not share the trials of this time with my people. Christians in Germany will face the terrible alternative of either willing the defeat of their nation in order that Christian civilization may survive, or willing the victory of their nation and thereby destroying our civilization. I know which of those alternatives I must choose; but I cannot make this choice in security."

His life personified service, commitment and costly grace. In fact, the day before he was executed, he counseled widows of those who were executed for plotting the death of Hitler, He felt that he could ease their debilitating depression and anxiety.

And his message for all of us — not just Christians — should be reaffirmed.

Within our secular world we are falling for messages that promise much, but require little of us in return. We want more government services, but no tax increases. We want our highways and bridges fixed, but don't want to pay for them. We want clean air, but don't want to make personal sacrifices to make it happen.

We want cheap grace because costly grace means personal hardships.

Bonhoeffer thought it imperative that we change our ways.

We need to pay attention — before it's too late!

Aging and maturity

There is no question that many of us are old.

But there may well be a question whether we are mature.

I recently heard an elderly man complain about his lot in life. He has a collective memory for depressing negatives and a rich vocabulary describing how miserable he is. His grandchildren are ungrateful, unloving and "don't appreciate what I've done for them."

They rarely visit him, he said. I can understand why. Who wants to be around an old grouch? Or expose young children to him?

Clearly he is an old man. But I wouldn't call him mature. His outlook on life reflects that of a self-centered, spoiled youngster who failed to receive all the gifts he thought he deserved for his birthday.

My encounter with him prompted me to think about the differences between being mature and being old. So, here are my impressions about mature folks and the nature of maturity—descriptions that I wouldn't necessarily apply to old people.

• Mature people are alive to the wonder and curiosity they experienced as a child, and retain the ability for childlike play.

• Maturity is carrying within you a new song every day.

• Maturity is knowing you are aging well when you no longer worry about getting old.

• Mature people pay attention to others who are aging well—and learn from them.

• Mature people don't try to young anymore; they wear their age with pride.

• Maturity is appreciating how little you know.

• Maturity is realizing that other people's faults are no worse than yours. Old people focus on the flaws of others and overlook their own.

• Mature people realize that few, if any, of their favorite beliefs and ideas originated with them.

• Maturity is a commitment to personal growth, bolstered by a belief that learning is a key to living a fulfilling life.

• Mature people look at expensive antiques and remember, with a sparkle in their eyes, when they first bought stuff just like them.

• Mature people would not be characterized as self-centered or self-absorbed. They have little self-consciousness. They are at ease with their imperfect lives.

• Maturity is making a will, arranging for their death, and then baking a meatloaf, cleaning the bedrooms, and in all other ways, getting on with

203

their life.

• Mature people view aging as an inevitable process, best managed by those who are not faint of heart.

And maturity is appreciating the wisdom offered to us by two of my favorite people:

Bernard Baruch—"To me, old age is fifteen years older than I am."

• Erma Bombeck—"Big deal! I'm used to dust!" (Requested for her gravestone.)

Life goals

"I hope my retirement years will be happy."

"I believe my retirement years will be fulfilling."

"I am convinced my retirement years will be enjoyable."

Hopes, beliefs and convictions.

Some of us live lives filled with hopes. "I hope to accumulate enough savings to give my children a good education." "I hope to live a long life." "I hope to write a book when I retire."

There is nothing wrong with hopes. We all have them. But are they enough? Can a fulfilling life be built on hopes?

Not likely. Hoping something will come true won't make it happen. It's like wishing on a star; sounds good, but stars have no history of delivering wishes.

What about beliefs? "I believe I can be successful." "I believe I can accumulate enough savings to give my children a good education." "I believe I can live a long, productive life."

Will beliefs make a desired future happen? If one believes strongly enough will one's wishes and dreams come true? Probably not. This isn't to say that the beliefs we have are unimportant. Of course they are. But in themselves, they do not have the power insure success, accumulate savings or prolong life.

But surely convictions are enough to make good things happen. "I will enjoy my retirement years." "They will be fulfilling and enjoyable."

Haven't we been taught that we must possess convictions in order to reach our goals? What good is this lesson if it doesn't produce desired results?

It's questions like these that reveal the limitations of hopes, beliefs and convictions.

We have been taught since we were very young that hope somehow brings rewards. "Make a wish," we counsel youngsters. "If you want it badly enough, your wish will come true." And all of us hoped it would.

What about beliefs? Same game! "Believe in yourself and you can do anything." When I was young, I believed that parents and adults believed that. I've since learned differently.

Ah, but convictions. Surely if one's conviction is strong enough to make something happen, it will. "If you really want to go to college, you can." "If you really want to live a long life, you can do it." Sounds seductive, doesn't it?

Again, conviction is important, if not critical, to the accomplishment of goals.

But there is something more that is needed. And my experience is that we are downplaying, even ignoring, this critical factor. Maybe because it's so tough and requires so much of us — or our children.

It's the missing link in accomplishment. It's the final straw in achieving lofty goals. It's the single factor without which goals, beliefs and convictions will lie dormant.

It is disciplined action!

Nothing moves us from lofty words and cherished, passionate thoughts but this. It's the difference between talking a good game and playing a great one. In other words, action without discipline is unlikely to result in significant accomplishment. Without discipline a person's actions may spin in circles, or head off in irregular patterns, or fly this way and that.

While not undermining the importance of hopes, beliefs and convictions, let's be sure we counsel ourselves — and especially children — that worthwhile goals and accomplishments can only be achieved through disciplined action.

And let's be honest — that means hard, rigorous effort with little chance of shortcuts. Hopes, beliefs and convictions are more likely to reach fruition when hard work is involved.

Understanding why they do it

When confronted with questions and uncertainty about the human condition, and specifically, why an individual would commit such a heinous act against innocent people — such as the latest murders of worshipers in a Texas church or the shootings in Las Vegas — I often turn to reread books written by Eric Hoffer, a former longshoreman, philosopher and college professor. He was awarded the Presidential Medal of Freedom in 1983. Here are a few of his thoughts from his book, "The Passionate State of Mind."

"A fateful process is set in motion when the individual is released to the freedom of his own impotence and left to justify his existence by his own efforts. The autonomous individual, striving to realize himself and prove his worth, has created all that is great in literature, art, music, science and technology.

"The autonomous individual, also, when he can neither realize himself nor justify his existence by his own efforts, is a breeding call of frustration, and the seed of the convulsions which shake our world to its foundations.

"The individual on his own is stable only so long as he is possessed of self-esteem. The maintenance of self-esteem is a continuous task which taxes all of the individual's powers and inner resources. We have to prove our worth and justify our existence anew each day. When, for whatever reason, self-esteem is unattainable, the autonomous individual becomes a highly explosive entity. He turns away from an unpromising self and plunges into the pursuit of pride — the explosive substitute for self-esteem. All social disturbances and upheavals have their roots in crises of individual self-esteem, and the great endeavor in which the masses most readily unite is basically a search for pride.

"It is by its promise of a sense of power that evil often attracts the weak.

"It has often been said that power corrupts. But it is perhaps equally important to realize that weakness, too, corrupts. Power corrupts the few, while weakness corrupts the many.

"Hatred, malice, rudeness, intolerance, and suspicion are the fruits of weakness. The resentment of the weak does not spring from any injustice done to them, but from the sense of their inadequacy and impotence. They hate not wickedness but weakness.

"We are prone to sacrifice others when we are ready to sacrifice ourselves."

Wellbeing

Remember that old saw, "We are our own worst enemy?"
Well, there is some evidence that we are.

For oldsters like me, we have pretty well lived our lives. It's unlikely we will be making any major changes in who we are or what we do in the remaining years. But we may be able to impact the lives of our children or grandchildren by sharing some consequential information with them.

As long-time readers of my columns can likely guess, I have read another book about human behavior. It's titled "Well Being" and it's about the lives you and I are living and what we have done that has made our lives worthwhile and the decisions we have made that have been either misguided or just plain wrong.

Contrary to what many people believe, well-being isn't just about being happy. Nor is it about being wealthy or successful. And it's not limited to physical health and wellness. In fact, focusing on any of these elements in isolation could drive us to feelings of frustration and even failure.

A Gallup research project conducted a global study of people in more than 150 countries. They concluded that there are five universal elements of well-being that differentiate a thriving life from one spent suffering.

The first element is about how we occupy our time in the world of work: Career Wellbeing.

Secondly it is about relationships including the love in our lives: Social Wellbeing.

Thirdly is about how effectively we manage our economic life: Financial Wellbeing.

Fourth is about having good health and our ability to get things done on a daily basis: Physical Wellbeing.

The fifth element is about the sense of engagement we have where we live: Community Wellbeing.

This massive Gallup study found that 66 percent of the people are doing well in at least one of these areas but just 7 percent are thriving in all five. Further, if we are struggling in any one of these elements — and most of us are — it damages our wellbeing and wears on our daily lives. When we strengthen our wellbeing in any of these areas we will improve our lives.

The study also found that for many people, spirituality or a deep commitment — such as protecting the environment — inspires and enhances their daily lives.

However, the biggest single threat to our wellbeing tends to be ourselves. We allow short-term decisions to override what's best for our long-term wellbeing. If we can find short-term incentives that are consistent with our long-term objectives, we are likely to make the right decisions in the moment.

Of special interest is a huge appendix which presents wellbeing data (Thriving, Struggling or Suffering) in the world's countries and in cities and states in the U.S. Arizona ranks 21st in the Thriving category; Hawaii is first. With regard to countries, Denmark and Finland are the top two with the United States checking in at 19.

Some thoughts for graduating classes

This is the season for graduations and commencement addresses. It's been years since I spoke at a high school graduation but if I were to give another one it would likely include some of the following thoughts.

• I hope each of you will live a successful life. But of more importance, I believe, is to lead a valuable life. To become a person whose life has value for others is our highest calling.

• Your character, decency and compassion will become increasingly important as you age. I urge you to prioritize their development.

• I hope you discover what really matters in life and that you never forget it.

• One critical sign of maturity is reaching a point in your life when you are no longer primarily governed by what others think of you; you feel reasonably satisfied with yourself and your self-development.

• I hope you soon learn that to understand others is directly related to the degree that you understand yourself.

• High among the most important lessons in life that is critical to your development is to understand the meaning of love. It is best to approach this lesson unselfishly, patiently and with a sense of wonder.

• The more you are exposed to kindness and love, the kinder and more loving you will become.

• There is, in most people, human decency. Look for it. It will most often be found in those who truly care for others.

• One sigh of maturity us when you achieve success without depriving others of their successes.

• Try to understand that intelligence is no guarantee of wisdom, nor does sensitivity mean you will be more compassionate toward others. Intent, purpose and commitment must be factored into these equations. I believe you will find that compassion is more critical to your development as a human being than intelligence.

• Treat people the way you would like to be treated and you will always have caring friends.

• To truly enjoy your life, work at developing a sense of humor. No matter how well it works for you today, it will become more essential and critical as you confront the challenges of tomorrow.

Learn to appreciate whimsy, irony, comedy and buffoonery which you will observe in the human condition. And learn to laugh…frequently, and with gusto. Your mental and emotional health is at stake.

Becoming and being a couple

They were senior adults, slowly walking around the courthouse plaza, talking to each another, holding hands, and smiling.

This wonderful expression of love and companionship wasn't lost on several of us who watched them from our benches.

Later that day, I sat down at my computer to record a few thoughts about this lovely couple. I reflected on the issues a married couple, who have been together for years, must have focused on and sometimes "overcome" in adapting themselves to each other.

I don't have space in my column to fully elaborate so I'll be as succinct as possible in identifying issues that most couples who remain committed to each other – whether they know it or not – are likely to have dealt with successfully. Of course, I know one marriage far better than any others, so I'll use ours as an example.

• The gender issue: men and women are different. The wise learn to celebrate those differences.

• Birth order: My Beloved had an older brother; I was an only child. She knew how to handle me, often making me feel that I was in charge.

• Right brain/left brain: I was way right, she was substantially left. After several years of wondering why we differed so often, we read a book on this topic and quickly found the positives that collaboration could bring us.

• Extrovert/Introvert: She was the former, I am the latter. She helped bring me out of "my shell" and gave me the love and confidence to become comfortable opening myself to others.

• Lark/Owl: She was a morning person, I preferred the night. We decided to enjoy both and respect the other's predilection.

• Interests/Goals: While different in the early years, they gradually came together. We became "one!"

• Religious beliefs: She grew up a Southern Baptist and I was a Presbyterian. We attended different protestant churches throughout our lives until she became a Unitarian Universalist in her later years. From Baptist to UU can certainly be called a significant "leap of faith!"

• Educational differences: Both of us were college-educated with advanced degrees and smart enough to share a deep love for learning and reading books.

• Age differences: Less than a year separated us and was never an issue.

• Political differences: They didn't exist. We were as one!

• The morale curve: I learned about this significant psychological principle – and the one in the following paragraph – when I was on the staff of the Menninger Foundation, a psychiatric center in Topeka, Kansas. I regard these two descriptors of human behavior as the most important I have ever come across. The curve illustrates the ups and downs a person experiences when making a role change of any kind: e.g. a new job, new parent, new relationship, new home, new assignment. It reflects the underlying psychological processes that occur when we lose the supportive structures we are accustomed to.

• Psychological contracts: These are the hidden roots under every interpersonal exchange. These contracts are unwritten, nonverbal, and often unconscious expectations that underlie each relationship we have. They constitute what we expect of another person. But since they are unspoken and unwritten, it's unlikely the other person is aware of them. The violation of a "contract" could cause a couple considerable frustration and even harm. Somehow My Beloved and I managed to bring these out into the open early in our relationship and avoided the misunderstandings and conflicts that are often major factors in marriages and divorces.

In my book, Lessons for Leaders, which I wrote in 2005, there is a more detailed examination of the morale curve and psychological contracts. If interested, copies of the book are in the Prescott Public Library, on the main level near the Librarians' desk. You can check one out or read it there. Copies are also in the Prescott College Library. Or perhaps you know someone who was (or is) enrolled in the Prescott Area Leadership program who will lend you their copy of the book. I believe you will find these two chapters of considerable interest.

A few thoughts on not growing up

I acknowledge that I am old.

But I am steadfastly confident that I am not finished "growing-up."

There is still more to come, more lessons to learn.

Some folks assume they are grown-ups when they are in their 20s or 30s, while others are excited to continue growing up for the remainder of their lives.

Adolescent behavior, unexamined beliefs and child-like attitudes are characteristics of adults who, to paraphrase the words of French literacy historian Charles Augustin Sainte-Beuve, "permitted their clocks to stop at a certain point in their lives."

One wonders if they believe they "have arrived" and thus have nothing else to learn about themselves or of the world they inhabit. Perhaps they are unmindful of the proverb "It's what you learn after you know it all that counts."

Those persons who choose to stop learning fail at growing up. They live their lives well below their potential. Some acknowledge that life defeated them; problems overwhelmed their abilities to cope. Others are seduced by easy, simplistic answers to complex questions, discovering they are ill-equipped to deal with the tough realities of life.

Whatever the reason, complacency, indifference, rigidity or a willing imprisonment in comfortable habits and unexamined opinions identify their lives. They cannot escape their past, for one reason or another. Thus they are unable to live in the present or explore the future—two prerequisites for growing up.

Growing up means continuing to deal with the cards life hands us. We grow up as we confront life's inevitable losses, learn from our mistakes as we mature in our ability to love and share, as we continue to take risks, and as we learn to live with decisions and choices we cannot change.

Growing up means we continue to accumulate information and skills, adapting ourselves to new technology, discoveries and inventions. We grow up as we learn to minimize distress and handle stress. We grow up as we learn to handle successfully commitments and roles we have either chosen or had to assume.

Growing up means we accept—if not celebrate—the fact that life is a continuous unfolding and endless process of self-discovery. The challenge is to match our personalities and abilities against the situations life presents us.

Growing up means we do not lock ourselves into the prison of preoccupation. Rather, we continue to be curious about life, interested in exploring new worlds and discovering different ways of improving ourselves.

It means, perhaps most of all, that we are excited about being lifelong learners.

I don't want ever to feel I have grown up. Fortunately, my good friends assure me this should never be a problem.

I hope your friends feel the same way about you!

For all the children

I lease to you, my children, for the duration of your stay on this tumultuous, rolling ball —

LAUGHTER, which I beseech you to use continuously and with abandon.

ENERGY, which I hope will be in full supply for the rest of your lives.

COMPASSION, which I urge you to nurture and share wherever and whenever you feel it can help.

LOVE, which I trust you will replenish then give away with no thought of your own need.

PRIDE, which I encourage you to develop in order to share with those who need more.

STRENGTH, so that you can carry on when adversity threatens.

IDEALISM, which enables you to withstand the common realities that try to trample your beliefs.

SPONTANEITY, which gives you permission to be yourself, even as you question your identity.

SUCCESS, in whatever you decide is your definition, regardless of society's characterization.

JOY, for which you must find your own resources so that tomorrow you can extend it to others.

APPRECIATION, of diversity and similarities, but mostly of the qualities of humanness that draw people together.

TOLERANCE, which enables you to love those you dislike while appreciating differences that make each of us unique.

INTEGRITY, which makes inner consistency the basis for healthy living.

LEARNING, which you must continue if you are to combat creeping ignorance that threatens all lives.

I encourage you to assault windmilled resignation and indifference with a Quixotic lance, so that the dragons of hate and prejudice are diminished, if not banished from our kingdom.

Thoughts on mental health

Many moons ago in the land of wheat and hills (Kansas), I served on the staff of The Menninger Foundation, a psychiatric facility in Topeka.

While the primary thrust of the large campus-like institution was assisting individuals to overcome challenges to their mental health, of equal concern was to help them achieve mentally healthy approaches to life.

In developing these positive approaches, two psychologists asked 14 of their colleagues to describe five people whom they considered to be mentally/emotionally healthy men and women. Approximately 80 individuals were identified. The two researchers then sought to find common qualities within these individuals. They discovered five characteristics that, they concluded, identified mentally/emotionally healthy persons.

First, these people were able to treat others as individuals. They didn't categorize people. They were able to see the uniqueness of each person and could open themselves to the rich variety that different people offer.

Second, the individuals had a variety of sources of gratification. All of their psychological needs were not in one basket. They had a number of ways of enjoying themselves, of having fun and getting personal satisfaction.

Third, these people were flexible under stress. They could cope with problems in a number of different ways. When one method of solving a problem didn't work, they would try another tack. They could adapt strategies that enabled them to find alternative solutions to problems.

Fourth, the individuals were able to identify their strengths and accept their limitations. They did not depreciate their abilities and talents nor overvalue themselves.

And last, mentally healthy people were active and productive in a quality manner. They were active because they enjoyed what they were doing while their productive activities afforded them pleasure.

It's important to understand that being a mentally healthy person is never a static condition. Each of us is always in the process of becoming mentally healthy as opposed to having arrived.

Need a little help in becoming a mentally healthy person? Dr. Karl Menninger, the late psychiatrist and author, gave us several guidelines that should be helpful:

• Set up as an ideal the facing of reality as honestly and as cheerfully as possible.

• Cultivate social contacts and culture developments.

• Recognize neurotic evasions as such and substitute hobbies for habits when needed.

• Learn to recognize the symptoms of your mental problems and how best to deal with them.

• Assume that the unhappy are always (at least partly) wrong.

I have a suggestion that I would add to the above list: Develop an active sense of humor. It has bailed me out of numerous challenging – and potentially negative – situations.

The human condition

It goes somewhat like this: An old friend asks how and what I am doing, and in the course of replying I mention that I am still writing a column for The Courier. "What do you write about?" "Whatever I want to, I reply, but most of the columns fall under the heading of 'The Human Condition'."

That response usually shuts down the conversation. I'm not sure they know — or want to know — what I mean by "The Human Condition," and sometimes I'm not too clear on it either. However, today's column is certainly in that category. So, if you want an example, then you might want to read on. It's possible you may learn something about yourself.

All of us know that we have a personality. And most of us are aware that sometimes it works well for us. We're in control of our behavior and everything is going good. But we are also aware there are those times when we feel off keel and emotionally upset. Well, when that happens here are a few considerations to keep in mind.

First, your behavior doesn't occur by chance. All behavior is either motivated by you (your personality) or the environment. What you choose to do is a result of these two forces. Your responses do not occur accidentally.

Secondly, it's your task to maintain balance. When emotional storms buffet you about, it's your challenge to correct the list and ride out the storm. The more energy you expend getting your equilibrium back, the less you'll have to move ahead.

Thirdly, there will be times in your life when you will be emotionally disturbed. Whether you got up on the wrong side of the bed, or are feeling blue, or are upset by some real or perceived slight by someone, you are going to have periods when you feel hopeless or helpless.

Fourth, just because you are mildly disturbed emotionally doesn't mean you need professional help. When you have a cold it doesn't mean you're going to get pneumonia. Even if you get pneumonia, present treatment enables most people to recover. The same is true of mental illness. The difference between mild and severe is one of degree.

Finally, we are imperfect individuals. None of us grew up in a perfect environment or with a perfect heredity. Each of us has fragile spots. When the forces around us center on our weaknesses we'll have problems. We'll display symptoms of mental illness.

So, here's the good news: The late psychiatrist William Menninger indicated that the incidence of mental illness is one in one. All of us at times are mentally ill. In other words, it's normal to be a tad whacko at times. That ought to make you feel better about yourself, or your spouse, or your Uncle Ed.

It's when the forces impacting on us become more than we can handle that we ought to be concerned. Then we should seek professional help. The question then is, where do you find a good therapist? Like you find a good physician, through word of mouth or friends. There are a number of well-qualified therapists practicing here. Check out their credentials and don't be hesitant to ask for a no-charge interview to see if the rapport between the two of you is positive.

Good therapists are worth their weight in gold.

Reflections on our community

When our family first moved here in 1968, I considered Prescott—rightly or wrongly—to be a town. When we retired here in 1985, this beautiful community had become a city.

It was also a community that revered its history. Citizens who had lived here for years were proud of what Prescott once was and had become. Of course, some old-timers would fuss about the many changes that had taken place and the lack of appreciation for Prescott's rich frontier history as well as the stories that made this community unique.

But I would argue that most of the old-timers and the new residents appreciated the values, goals, ideas and ideals that community leaders developed and accepted.

What has emerged through the years has been a commitment to celebrate our history while adapting to the inevitable challenges that come from an increasing population.

I believe there is a recognition that certain covenants are important to us. There is a belief that the individual counts; that our natural resources should be preserved; that education and recreation are community priorities; that the community's history and stories should be appreciated; that the unique hometown character of the community should not be lost as population increases, and that the community's future should be tied to our past.

Prescott has many imbedded heroes and stories that identify the complex character of the community. There are myths, legends, characters and memories that tell us more than what history books relate.

Through them we learn about local adventurers and adventures, good and bad men (and women), controversy and harmony, noble and ignoble uses of power, roles leading families and elected officials played, and why certain ideas work here and others don't. It is the accumulation of these stories interwoven with history that enables us to understand Prescott's present culture.

To become part of the community newcomers should take the time and make the effort to appreciate the covenants that bind us and the culture that defines the community.

They might tour the Sharlot Hall Museum, read Melisa Ruffner's book, "Prescott: A Pictorial History," visit the Phippen Museum of Western Art, explore volunteer opportunities, take advantage of learning

programs offered through Yavapai and Prescott colleges. I also suggest folks apply to become involved in the Prescott Area Leadership program.

There is a lot going on here in our community. In the immortal words of Harry Golden, "Enjoy, enjoy!"

A brief look at growing older

This aging process is inescapable, isn't it?

Here in the Prescott area I see so many folks who are handling the aging process in healthy ways. Not so for all of the folks I meet, however. Some individuals appear to be conflicted about the process of growing old—and, perhaps, up!

A commitment to deny the inevitable process of aging isn't so much a surrender to the "cult of youth" as it is an ambivalence about self and what it means to be growing old and how one should handle this inexorable reality.

In thinking about this—as I must at my age—I have begun to suspect there may be two primary ways one approaches the specter of aging.

By facing forward or backward.

I've observed that a segment of the aging population confronts today by focusing on yesterday. They talk about past triumphs and tragedies, share memories of earlier events, recall long-ago happenings, and seem cheerful when their minds are imbedded in "happier" times. Some who cling to the illusions of youth are likely conflicted about accepting today as a positive transition to tomorrow.

If narcissism—an excessive interest in self, comfort, appearance—is indeed a dominant emphasis within society, as many critics argue, then an irrational terror of old age is understandable. Narcissistic personalities have few inner resources, depend on others to validate their sense of self, and need to be admired for their beauty, handsomeness, charm and power. Obviously, these attributes tend to fade as they age.

Narcissists not only take little interest in the future, but are often unprepared to deal with it since they cannot visualize themselves as being anything but young, vibrant and admired.

Facing resolutely backward in order to sustain their youth is an unsatisfactory way to cope with the daily exigencies of aging. Regarding old age as intolerable often leads to irrational panic.

The second alternative of facing forward makes more sense. Rather than loathing the aging process, the realist comes to accept it, preferring to look at the future as filled with opportunities for continued growth, service and personal fulfillment.

Those who have come to grips with aging have developed a perspective toward life and themselves that is based on the belief that they are contributors.

They are likely to be active in their community, engaged in staying healthy and alert, committed to learning how best to live fully despite age-imposed limitations, and are enthusiastic about sharing their love with their families or friends.

While aging contributors are aware that technological changes may render much of their knowledge obsolete, they also know that wisdom only comes to those with years of experience who are committed learners and who are seeking to make a positive difference in their communities.

In addition, a number of aging contributors use their knowledge to guide younger men and women to become active, contributing citizens in a world desperate for commitment to ideals, not just involvement in life.

Perhaps above all else, the aging contributors I admire are dreamers. Primarily, I believe, because the dreamers of the world have held onto their idealism. I have yet to meet a contributor, regardless of age, who is not an idealist.

An idealist will age, but never grow old!

Keep it up, you Prescott dreamers!

Thinking and being transitional

When I resigned from The Menninger Foundation in the mid-'70s, I started the first of several companies. I named it "Transitions, Inc." Why?

Because we are transitional human beings.

Because living is an interim adventure, between two great personal events, birth and death.

We are between times, between ages, between rites of passage.

In transition, we pass from one day, week, month, year to another, realizing that in this constant process of moving from the past to the present to the future, we never get it quite right. It's not easy determining where we have been, where we are, and where we wish to go and why.

In this context, we appreciate the statement, "I lived half my life before I discovered it was a do-it-yourself job!"

What we begin to understand is that all of us are getting on-the-job training. We are in the midst of history and no matter what will come, there will be little time for rehearsals. Life is a constant work in progress.

We begin to understand that one of the most important questions before us is where we fit in the great scheme of things. And many of us recall the Charlie Brown strip where, confused about life, he consults Lucy at her psychiatric booth. She tells him life is like a deck chair on a cruise ship. Passengers open up the canvas chairs so they can sit in the sun.

"Some people," she says, "place their chairs facing the rear of the ship so they can see where they've been. Other people face their chairs forward; they want to see where they're going."

Looking sternly at him, she says, "On the cruise ship of life, which way is your deck chair facing?" He answers, "I've never been able to get one unfolded."

Well, most of us have found ways to get one ready to sit in. We're wrestling with the direction to face. And that isn't always a crystal clear choice.

But that fork, and probably every other one, has been taken before. We stand on others' shoulders whose lives make us taller than we think we are. Many are no longer with us, but something of their lives remains within us. What they saw and learned and experienced gives us a particular vision.

This is what John Cheever calls the "continuousness of life." We are interim, transitional creatures, but we are also part of a great stream of humanity. Who we are — and what we bring, unrehearsed, to this great play called life — does not disappear. Others can, and perhaps will, stand on our shoulders.

224

So, in our interim state, let's not sell ourselves short. We may have complex questions about where we are and where we're going, but let's not be too hard on ourselves. I suspect there has been considerable meaning in what we have done, are doing, and will do.

Maybe we should spend less time trying to turn back the clock and more time winding it up again.

Notes & Credits

I'm one of the newest members of the Ron Barnes fan club, meeting Ron in his 90th year and through interesting circumstances as part of his hospice team. I don't remember how it started, but word got back to me that Ron wanted to write a column about the importance of hospice care and how it was helping him. He wasn't sure where to start and needed more information so he could write a good piece for his upcoming Daily Courier column.

He graciously invited me to his home and asked me questions about how I ended up in Prescott and what I had done with my life so far. And we talked about his 31 years as a Daily Courier columnist, what Prescott Area Leadership (PAL) is, how the idea for the Hungry Kids project took root during his time in the Korean War, and much he missed his beloved wife, Betsy.

Later that week, I had the honor of helping put together what would be his final column, sharing the news with his longtime readers that he was on hospice, but like the educator he is, explaining and demystifying what it meant. He liked the way I wrote some of the paragraphs I had sent him and invited me to his house again to talk about whether I'd consider writing a column for the Daily Courier, if he put in a good word with the editorial staff.

I learned he was working on a book of his favorite columns, with the help of two good friends and PAL graduates, Patt Parker and Alex Piacenza. I mentioned I had helped a few folks publish their memoirs on Amazon and offered to share some tips. A few days later, the four of us met and suddenly I was writing a column for the Daily Courier AND editing Ron's book.

And that's how it happens when you get to know Ron Barnes—you find yourself pushing beyond what you imagined possible while still being incredibly grateful at the same time. (I suspect many PAL graduates would back me up on this!) With the immense support of Patt and Alex, we sifted through the columns of the last seven years, picking out the best ones with Ron's approval and assembling them into the book you just read. Patt's granddaughter, Aspen Herzog, who graduated with a degree in studio art and is a freelance illustrator, kindly donated her time and created the wonderful pen and ink drawings to illustrate the three sections of the book and give those pages some extra flair. Daughter Lisa Barnes and grandson Dylan Clark sent photos we could use for the cover and for the Granddaddyism section.

I am pleased to share at the time of this book's publication in May 2021, Ron's hanging in there and looking forward to his 91st birthday this summer. We all hope he will be sharing his great sense of humor with us for many months to come.

Whether it's your first time reading Ron's columns, or you're a Daily Courier subscriber who has enjoyed his wit and wisdom through the years, a big thank you from all of us for reading this book and supporting the Ron and Betsy Barnes Youth Scholarship Foundation.

Gratefully,
Kelly Paradis, editor